COPYRIGHT PAGE

Copyright © 2024 by Sage Everest

This is a work of nonfiction. The names and identifying details of individuals mentioned in personal stories have been changed to protect their privacy.

Published by Kindle Direct Publishing 2024.

Printed in the United States of America.

EMBRACING FEAR AS A CATALYST FOR GROWTH

Table of Contents:

ACKNOWLEDGMENTS

Writing this book has been a profoundly transformative journey that has required more vulnerability, reflection, and self-discovery than I could have imagined. As much as it is my story, this book is also a collective effort that would not have been possible without the support, love, and encouragement of many incredible people.

First and foremost, I want to express my deepest gratitude to my family. To my children, your unconditional love and presence in my life inspire me daily. You've taught me more about courage and vulnerability than any life lesson ever could. I am incredibly proud of who you are and all that you continue to become.

To my close friends, who have listened to my doubts, supported my dreams, and helped me face my fears—I owe you more than words can say. Thank you for holding space for me and reminding me that even in moments of uncertainty, I am never alone.

I want to thank my mentor and guide, Rachel Smith, who helped me find my voice during times of uncertainty. Your wisdom and guidance gave me the confidence to continue, even when the path was unclear.

To my editor and publishing team, your dedication and expertise helped bring this book to life. Thank you for your attention to detail, thoughtful feedback, and push to dig deeper. This book is better because of your insight and care.

Finally, thank you to the readers. Thank you for picking up this book, for trusting me to guide you through your journey of facing fear, and for allowing my words to become part of your life. I hope this book catalyzes your growth and helps you discover the strength, resilience, and courage that already exists within you.

This book was written with you in mind, and I share it with you with the deepest gratitude. May you always remember that fear is not the end of the road but the beginning of your transformation.

With love and gratitude,

Sage Everest

INTRODUCTION: EMBRACING FEAR AS A CATALYST FOR GROWTH

"Fear is not the enemy. It is the doorway to the life you have yet to create, the person you are meant to become, and the strength you have yet to realize."

We've all experienced fear in our lives. Whether it's fear of failure, rejection, or the unknown, these feelings can paralyze us and keep us from moving forward. Yet, what if fear wasn't something to be avoided or silenced? What if fear could be a guide—a catalyst for growth that transforms our lives in ways we never thought possible?

This book is not about eliminating fear. Fear is a natural part of the human experience, a signal that we are on the edge of something new that matters deeply to us. Instead, this book is about embracing fear and learning to see it for what it truly is: an opportunity for growth, transformation, and more profound self-discovery.

For years, I lived in the shadow of my fears. I feared making mistakes, being vulnerable, and stepping into the unknown. These fears kept me from fully experiencing life and connecting with the people I loved. I stayed in my comfort zone, believing that if I could avoid fear, I could avoid pain. But in doing so, I also avoided growth.

It wasn't until I began to face my fears—step by step, moment by moment—that I realized fear wasn't my enemy. It was my teacher. Every time I leaned into the discomfort of fear, I discovered a new layer of strength, resilience, and courage within myself. I learned that fear isn't something to run from; it's something to move through. And on the other side of that fear is a life that is richer, more meaningful, and more aligned with who I truly am.

In the pages of this book, I will share with you my journey of learning to embrace fear as a catalyst for growth. Through personal stories, practical exercises, and deep reflective wisdom, we will explore the many faces of fear—fear of vulnerability, fear of failure, fear of intimacy—and how these fears, when faced with courage, can lead to profound personal transformation.

This book is not just about my story; it's about yours. I hope that as you read, you will see your fears reflected in these pages and find the courage to embrace them. Whether you're facing fear in your relationships, career, or personal development, this book will guide you toward seeing fear as a doorway to more profound love, tremendous success, and a more authentic life.

Each chapter is designed to help you confront a different aspect of fear, whether it's the fear of conflict, the fear of being vulnerable, or the fear of letting go. Through reflection, storytelling, and actionable steps, you will be equipped to transform your relationship with fear and use it as a tool for growth.

This journey won't always be easy. There will be moments when fear feels overwhelming and stepping into the unknown is too complicated. But remember this: every time you face your fear, you grow stronger. Whenever you choose courage over comfort, you step toward becoming the person you are meant to be.

Let's embark on this journey together. Let's embrace fear, not as something to overcome but as something that will guide us to our most significant potential.

CHAPTER 1: SEEING FEAR AS A FRIEND

We've all been taught, directly or indirectly, that fear is something to conquer. We grow up believing that fear is a barrier between us and our dreams. I used to think that way, too; that fear was a wall I had to break through to succeed. But what if I told you that fear is not your enemy? Fear is your greatest ally, constant companion, and a wise teacher guiding you toward your fullest potential.

I remember a moment in my life, sitting in my office, staring at a blank screen, paralyzed by a decision that felt too big to handle. As a mental health professional, I was supposed to have all the answers. I was supposed to guide others through their emotional challenges, helping them navigate their fears. But here I was, struggling to move forward with my career, my relationships, and the delicate balance of motherhood. The fear of failure was so overwhelming that it felt like a heavy fog, clouding my ability to see a clear path ahead.

Maybe you've felt that too—the weight of a decision, the crushing pressure of expectations, the fear of not being enough. Fear manifests in many ways, yet we often respond to it similarly. We freeze. We avoid. We run away.

But what if, instead of seeing fear as something to escape, we embraced it? What if we saw fear not as a barrier but as a signal, a guidepost, pointing us toward the areas where we have the most significant potential for growth? This chapter will guide you through understanding and reframing fear, not as a foe to be defeated but as a friend who can lead you to the summit of your potential.

MY STORY: FEAR AS A CONSTANT COMPANION

I've never lived a life free from fear. And if I'm being honest with you—and myself—I don't think I ever will. Fear has always been there, lurking in the background in my work, relationships, and especially in raising my children. I thought the rest would disappear for years once I overcame one fear. But each time I climbed one metaphorical mountain, another, often taller and more intimidating, would appear on the horizon.

One of the most vivid examples of fear gripping my life came during a significant career transition. At that time, I was struggling to balance my role as a mental health professional with the demands of being a mother. The two worlds collided constantly. I would leave work feeling emotionally drained, only to walk into a home that required more of me than I sometimes thought I had gone to give. The fear of failing at both weighed on me every day. I feared being a bad therapist, and even more, I feared being a lousy mother. There were moments when I thought about quitting my job altogether to relieve myself of the constant pressure, the anxiety, and the fear of not being enough for my clients or my children.

I knew my fear well—it visited me every day. However, I didn't realize that this fear was not a signal that I was incapable or failing; it showed me where I needed to grow. The fear of not being enough wasn't something I needed to conquer—it was something I needed to understand. It told me I had more potential within myself than I was allowing myself to see.

YOUR FEAR: A MIRROR REFLECTING YOUR POTENTIAL

Take a moment and think about the fear that grips you the most. Is it the fear of failure? Fear of rejection? Fear of being vulnerable? Or maybe it's the fear of change, losing control, or not being good enough. Whatever it is, I want you to ask yourself: What is this fear trying to show me about myself?

You see, fear is not an arbitrary emotion that exists to torment us. In many ways, it is a mirror, reflecting the areas of our lives where we can grow most. The things we fear the most often hold the keys to our deepest desires and most significant potential.

If you fear failure, it's likely because success means much to you. Acceptance and belonging are vital to your sense of self if you fear rejection. If you fear vulnerability, it's because, deep down, you understand how much strength it takes to be open with others. Fear doesn't just reveal what you're afraid of—it shows what you care about most.

EXERCISE: IDENTIFYING YOUR FEAR

Here's a simple but powerful exercise to start reframing your relationship with fear:

1. **Write down your top three fears**. These could be related to your career, relationships, or personal life. Be honest and specific.

2. **Next to each fear, write down what you believe that fear is protecting you from**. For example, if your fear is public speaking, maybe it's protecting you from the potential embarrassment of failure or rejection.

3. **Now, reframe each fear as a signal**. What is this fear telling you about your growth potential? If you fear public speaking, perhaps it's because you can inspire others and lead, and your fear points you toward that opportunity for growth.

This exercise isn't about overcoming fear in one step—it's about starting to see fear as a friend, as something that points the way toward your highest potential.

A SHIFT IN PERCEPTION: THE POWER OF AWARENESS

When I first began this journey of reframing fear, I realized that the most significant shift happened when I became aware of my patterns. Before, I thought that fear was something to escape or suppress. It wasn't until I started paying attention to when and how fear showed up in my life that I began to see it for what it was—an invitation to step up, grow, and expand.

I remember a specific moment when this awareness hit me. I had been asked to present to a group of professionals at a conference —something I had done many times before. But this time was different. This time, I felt an overwhelming sense of inadequacy. I doubted whether I had anything valuable to say. What if I failed? What if I embarrassed myself? The fear was paralyzing.

But I stopped instead of running from that fear or letting it consume me. I took a deep breath and asked myself: *Why is this fear here?* I discovered that my fear wasn't irrational—it was pointing to something meaningful. I cared deeply about delivering value to the audience, and I feared not living up to the standards I had set for myself. My fear showed me the areas where I felt vulnerable and wanted to grow. It wasn't trying to hold me back; it was trying to guide me toward doing my best.

YOUR FEAR IS A MAP: IDENTIFYING GROWTH ZONES

Now, I want you to reflect on your own life. We often step into a growth zone when fear emerges. But because growth requires discomfort, our natural reaction is to avoid it. We stay in our comfort zones because it feels safe. But safety isn't where growth happens. Growth requires risk, uncertainty, and, yes, fear.

Think about the areas of your life where you feel the most fear. What is it that scares you? Is it a new opportunity at work that feels too big? Is it the fear of deepening a relationship and risking vulnerability? Is it the fear of pursuing a dream that seems out of reach?

Whatever it is, I want you to think of your fear as a map. Where does it point? What is it leading you toward?

Instead of asking, *"Why am I so afraid?"* ask, *"What is this fear trying to teach me?" This shift in mindset is the key to unlocking your potential. Fear is not a dead end—it's* a signpost pointing you toward the areas where you can experience the most growth.

EXERCISE: CREATING YOUR FEAR MAP

Let's make this tangible with a practical exercise. Grab a notebook or a piece of paper and create your "Fear Map." This exercise will help you identify where fear is showing up and how it can guide you toward growth.

1. **List Your Top 3 Fears**: List the three things that scare you the most. These could be related to your career, relationships, or personal life.

   - For example:
     - Fear of speaking up in meetings.
     - Fear of starting a new career path.
     - Fear of deepening a relationship.

2. **Identify the Growth Opportunity**: Next to each fear, write down the potential growth opportunity it represents. What is this fear pointing you toward? What area of your life might improve if you leaned into this fear?

   - Example:
     - Fear of speaking up in meetings → Opportunity to develop leadership skills.
     - Fear of starting a new career path → Opportunity to pursue a passion and build a fulfilling career.
     - Fear of deepening a relationship → Opportunity to experience emotional connection and intimacy.

3. **Create a Small Action Step**: Write down one small step to confront each fear. This step should be manageable—something that pushes you slightly outside your comfort zone but isn't overwhelming.

   ○ Example:
      - Fear of speaking up in meetings → Speak once during a small team meeting this week.
      - Fear of starting a new career path → Research one potential career change or contact someone in that field for advice.
      - Fear of deepening a relationship → Share one vulnerable thought or feeling with someone close to you.

As you work through this exercise, remember that the goal isn't to eliminate fear. The goal is to use it as a guide. Fear shows you where your opportunities for growth lie—lean into it, step by step.

LEARNING TO DANCE WITH FEAR

We often think of fear as something we need to defeat. We picture ourselves as warriors, fighting against fear, pushing through it with sheer willpower. But what if we learned to dance with fear instead of fighting fear?

This realization changed everything for me. Fear is like a partner in a dance—it will always be there, moving with you and guiding your steps. If you fight against it, you'll stumble. But if you learn to move with it, to flow with its rhythm, you'll find that it leads you in the right direction.

One of the most profound shifts in my life came when I stopped trying to conquer fear and started learning to embrace it. I stopped seeing it as a force to be overcome and began to see it as a force that could shape me, refine me, and ultimately help me grow.

I remember a time when I was faced with a difficult decision at work. A new opportunity had presented itself—with more responsibility, visibility, and, of course, more pressure. The fear of taking on this role was overwhelming. What if I wasn't ready? What if I failed in front of my colleagues? The temptation to say no, to stay in my safe, familiar role, was strong.

But then I asked myself: *What if this fear is exactly what I need? What if this fear is trying to show me that I am ready for more?*

Instead of pushing the fear away, I allowed myself to sit with it. I listened to what it was trying to tell me. I recognized that the fear wasn't there to stop me—it was there to guide me toward a new level of growth.

PRACTICAL TOOLS: LIVING IN ALIGNMENT WITH FEAR

To start dancing with fear instead of fighting it, you need to practice acknowledging and working with your fears daily. Here are a few practical tools you can integrate into your life:

1. **Daily Fear Check-In**: Each morning or evening, take a few minutes to reflect on where fear showed up that day. Ask yourself:

   - *What was I afraid of today?*
   - *How did I respond to that fear?*
   - *What opportunity for growth did that fear present?* This practice will help you become more aware of how fear guides you and how you can learn to move with it rather than resist it.

2. **Mindful Breathing When Fear Arises**: When fear shows up, it often triggers a fight-or-flight response. To counteract this, practice mindful breathing. When you feel fear arising, please take a deep breath, hold it for a moment, and then exhale slowly. Repeat this a few times, allowing your body to calm down and your mind to focus. This practice helps you pause and reflect on what your fear is trying to tell you before reacting impulsively.

3. **Embrace the "What If"**: Fear often thrives on the "what if" question. But instead of letting those "what ifs" spiral into negative scenarios, turn them into possibilities for growth:

   - *What if this fear is showing me my next ample opportunity?*
   - *What if this fear is the key to unlocking a new chapter in my life?* This simple shift in mindset can transform the way you approach fearful situations.

REFLECTION: YOUR RELATIONSHIP WITH FEAR

Take a moment to reflect on your current relationship with fear. How have you been responding to it? Have you been fighting it, running from it, or ignoring it altogether? Or have you been listening to what it says, allowing it to guide you toward growth?

As you shift your perception of fear from an enemy to a friend, you will notice a profound shift in how you approach challenges. Fear will no longer be a force that paralyzes you but a signal that you are on the right path. The very presence of fear in your life is a sign that you are stepping outside of your comfort zone and moving toward something more significant.

Fear is not there to stop you. It's there to show you that you are capable of more than you realize.

MEMORABLE QUOTE:

"The fear you feel today is not a wall to stop you—it's a guide showing you the way to your greatest potential."

CHAPTER 2: CLIMBING THE MOUNTAIN OF SELF-DOUBT

Introduction: The Silent Thief of Dreams

"Self-doubt is the silent thief of dreams. It doesn't shout but whispers—telling you you're not ready, worthy, or enough."

We've all heard that voice, haven't we? That quiet, insidious whisper that plants seeds of doubt just as we're about to step into something bigger. It tells us to wait, hold back, and second-guess every decision. Self-doubt creeps in like a shadow, making our climb toward success feel steeper than it is.

But here's the truth: self-doubt does not reflect your abilities. It's a defense mechanism—a way fear tries to keep you from moving forward. And just like fear, self-doubt only shows up when you're on the verge of growth. It's a sign that you're stepping outside your comfort zone and moving toward something meaningful.

In this chapter, we're going to confront self-doubt head-on. We'll explore how it shows up, why it thrives on fear, and how to quiet its whispers so you can climb the mountain of your potential.

MY STORY: WHEN SELF-DOUBT NEARLY STOLE MY FUTURE

Let me tell you a story—one that's deeply personal. There was a moment in my career that should have been a turning point, a celebration of all the hard work I had put in. I had been offered a significant leadership role at my organization, one I had dreamed of for years. It was everything I had wanted—recognition, responsibility, the chance to make a real impact.

But the moment that offer was on the table, self-doubt began to whisper.

What if you're not ready? What if you fail? What if everyone realizes you're not good enough?

These thoughts were relentless, swirling in my mind day and night. Those doubts became so heavy that I seriously considered turning down the opportunity. After all, if I didn't leap, I couldn't fail.

But deep down, I knew that wasn't the truth. Turning down the offer wouldn't protect me—it would only confirm my self-doubt. It would keep me small, stuck, and safe. So, I decided to climb the mountain, even if I wasn't ready. I would take the role, face the challenges, and resolve my doubts.

And you know what? I succeeded. But not because I had no doubts—those never entirely went away. I succeeded because I decided to move forward despite them.

YOUR SELF-DOUBT: A LIAR IN DISGUISE

Now, let's talk about your self-doubt. You know the voice I'm talking about—the one that tells you that you're not good enough, experienced enough, or intelligent enough. That voice, the one that sounds so convincing, is nothing more than a liar in disguise.

Self-doubt is not the truth. It's not an accurate reflection of who you are or what you're capable of. It's a reaction to stepping into the unknown—a defense mechanism that tries to keep you from taking risks. But the irony is that self-doubt only appears when standing at the edge of something important. It shows up because you're about to grow, which is uncomfortable.

The key is not to eliminate self-doubt—because it will always try to find a way in—but to recognize it for what it is: a sign that you're on the right path.

EXERCISE: RECOGNIZING AND CHALLENGING SELF-DOUBT

To climb the mountain of self-doubt, you must first recognize when and where it appears. Let's do an exercise to help you identify the voice of self-doubt and challenge its lies.

1. **List Your Top 3 Doubts**: Start by writing down the top three doubts that hold you back. These could be doubts about your career, relationships, or personal goals. For example:

   - *I'm not qualified enough for this job.*
   - *I'm not good enough to pursue my passion.*
   - *I'm not deserving of love or success.*

2. **Question the Doubt**: Next, challenge each doubt by asking yourself:

   - *Is this true?*
   - *What evidence do I have that contradicts this doubt?*
   - *What would I tell a friend who had the same doubt?*

3. **Reframe the Doubt**: Now, rewrite each doubt as a positive affirmation supporting your growth. For example:

- *I am capable of learning and growing in this role.*
- *My passion is worth pursuing, and I am worthy of success.*
- *I deserve love and success as much as anyone else.*

This powerful exercise helps you see self-doubt for what it truly is: fear disguised as truth. The more you challenge it, the weaker it becomes.

SELF-DOUBT AND THE FEAR OF FAILURE: TWO SIDES OF THE SAME COIN

Let's examine one of the main drivers of self-doubt: the fear of failure. Self-doubt thrives on the idea that failure will somehow confirm our worst fears about ourselves. We think that if we fail, it will mean we are never good enough.

But that's not true.

Failure is not a reflection of your worth or abilities—it's a natural part of growth. Failure is one of the most valuable tools for learning and improvement. It teaches what doesn't work, sharpens your skills, and pushes you to grow in ways that success alone never could.

The most successful people in the world are not those who never failed—they're the ones who failed the most and kept going. They understood that failure was part of the journey, not a final destination.

PRACTICAL WISDOM: REDEFINING FAILURE ON YOUR TERMS

To overcome self-doubt, you need to redefine what failure means to you. Instead of seeing it as a verdict on your abilities, start seeing failure as feedback—a valuable guide that helps you adjust and improve.

1. **Failure as Feedback**: Each time you "fail," ask yourself, *What did I learn? How can I use this to grow?* Remember, every setback is an opportunity for improvement.

2. **Success as Progress, Not Perfection**: True success isn't about perfection but progress. It's about moving forward, even if the steps are small.

3. **Celebrate Your Effort**: Don't just celebrate the outcome—celebrate your effort. You defeat self-doubt every time you step toward your goal, even imperfectly.

EXERCISE: REDEFINING FAILURE AND SUCCESS

Let's take a moment to rewrite our definitions of success and failure. This will help us shift our mindset and weaken the grip that self-doubt has on us.

1. **Choose a Goal**: Write down a goal you've hesitated to pursue because of self-doubt. It could be something big, like changing careers, or something personal, like building deeper relationships.

2. **Redefine Success**: Now, redefine success to emphasize progress and effort, not perfection. For example:

   - *Success is taking one small step toward this goal every day.*
   - *Success is learning from each mistake and continuing to move forward.*

3. **Reframe Failure**: Next, redefine failure as part of the process. Write down how failure will serve as feedback, not a final judgment. For example:

   - *Failure is a lesson, not a verdict—part of my growth journey.*

This exercise will help you see success and failure in a new light. Self-doubt loses its power when you stop fearing failure and start embracing the learning process.

REFLECTION: CLIMBING HIGHER DESPITE DOUBT

Self-doubt is not the enemy—it's a challenge. It shows up precisely because you are stepping into something bigger, something that stretches you beyond your current limits. And that's a good thing.

The presence of self-doubt is not a sign that you should stop. It's a sign that you're growing. You don't need all the answers before taking the next step. You don't need to be free of doubt before you pursue your dreams.

It would be best if you were willing to climb the mountain, even with the doubts whispering in the background.

Because here's the truth: the higher you climb, the quieter those whispers will become. And when you reach the summit, you'll realize that self-doubt was never the truth—it was just a shadow cast by your brilliance.

MEMORABLE QUOTE:

"The presence of self-doubt is not a sign to stop—it's a signal that you're on the edge of something extraordinary."

CHAPTER 3: THE SUMMIT OF VULNERABILITY

Introduction: Vulnerability, the Courage to Be Seen

"Vulnerability is not about being weak—it's the courage to allow yourself to be seen for who you are."

We live in a world where vulnerability is often misunderstood. We're taught to equate vulnerability with weakness as if exposing our inner selves—our fears, insecurities, and flaws—will make us more susceptible to pain. But what if the opposite is true? What if vulnerability is the path to our most significant strength? What if it is the very thing that connects us, helps us grow, and leads us to deeper, more meaningful relationships?

I've spent years learning and unlearning what vulnerability means. For much of my life, I believed strength meant keeping things to myself, holding it all together, and projecting an image of competence. I was afraid that if I showed any cracks, people would judge me, reject me, or worse—think less of me. But over time, I learned that vulnerability is not a flaw. It is the most potent expression of courage we can offer the world.

Vulnerability is the summit of emotional bravery. Real connection begins when you stand open, let yourself be seen, and admit that you don't have all the answers. This chapter will explore why vulnerability is essential for personal growth, how it unlocks deeper relationships, and how to start practicing vulnerability.

MY STORY: THE MOMENT I LET MY GUARD DOWN

For years, I was the person who had it all together—or at least, that's what I wanted everyone to believe. As a mental health professional, I felt pressure to always be in control, to have the answers, to be the one others could lean on. And while I found purpose in helping others, I hid my struggles. I built walls around myself, thinking that was the only way to protect my heart. Vulnerability, to me, felt like a risk I couldn't afford to take.

Then came a time in my life when everything felt like falling apart. I was trying to balance the demands of my career with the responsibilities of raising my children. I was exhausted—emotionally and physically. But still, I told myself I couldn't let anyone see me struggling. I couldn't let anyone know how overwhelmed I felt because that would mean I wasn't as strong as I pretended to be.

But one evening, everything changed. Sensing something was wrong, a close friend asked me how I was doing. My instinct was to give the typical response: *"I'm fine, just busy."* But I hesitated. I felt the weight of everything I had been carrying, and for the first time in a long time, I allowed myself to be honest. I told her the truth—I was struggling. I felt like I was failing at everything: my career, my role as a mother, and even as a friend. I let the walls down and showed her the parts I had been hiding.

To my surprise, instead of judging me, she listened with empathy. She didn't offer quick solutions or dismiss my feelings; she held space for me to be vulnerable. In that moment, I realized that vulnerability wasn't weakness—it was what allowed me to connect deeply with another person. I felt lighter and stronger because I had allowed myself to be seen.

YOUR VULNERABILITY: A DOORWAY TO AUTHENTIC CONNECTION

Now, let's talk about your relationship with vulnerability. Think about the areas where you've built walls and avoid letting people see the real you. Maybe it's in your friendships where you keep conversations light and surface-level to prevent revealing your deeper feelings. Perhaps it's at work, where you feel pressure always to appear competent, never admitting when you're unsure or need help. Or maybe it's in your intimate relationships where you guard your heart because you fear rejection.

Vulnerability isn't about oversharing or exposing yourself indiscriminately. It's about allowing yourself to be accurate, even when uncomfortable. It's about acknowledging that you don't have to be perfect to be worthy of love, respect, or success. It's about choosing to show up fully, with all your imperfections, and trusting that who you are is enough.

When we allow ourselves to be vulnerable, we invite others to see the real us. And when others see the real us, something magical happens: we build more profound, more meaningful connections. Vulnerability is the key that unlocks empathy, understanding, and love. It is the foundation of true intimacy in our personal and professional lives.

EXERCISE: PRACTICING VULNERABILITY IN SMALL STEPS

Vulnerability doesn't have to be a grand gesture. Often, the small moments of openness have the most significant impact. Here's an exercise to help you practice vulnerability safely and flexibly.

1. **Identify a Safe Space**: Start by identifying one person in your life whom you trust—a friend, family member, or colleague. Vulnerability requires a foundation of trust, so choose someone who has shown empathy and support in the past.

2. **Share a Small Vulnerability**: In your following conversation with this person, choose to share something that makes you feel slightly uncomfortable. It could be a recent fear, mistake, or insecurity you've been carrying. Vulnerability doesn't mean revealing everything all at once—it's about being honest, even in small ways.

3. **Observe the Response**: How does the person respond after you share? Did they offer empathy? Did they listen without judgment? Most often, vulnerability strengthens relationships, creating deeper connections based on trust and understanding.

4. **Reflect**: Take a moment to reflect on how it felt to open up. What did you learn about yourself? How did it change your relationship with this person? Vulnerability is a practice; you build emotional resilience each time you engage.

This exercise is about practicing vulnerability in manageable, everyday moments. Over time, you'll see that vulnerability doesn't weaken you—it strengthens your relationships and your sense of self.

THE FEAR OF VULNERABILITY: WHY WE GUARD OURSELVES

So why is vulnerability so hard for us? Why do we build walls around ourselves, even when we crave connection and understanding?

At its core, the fear of vulnerability is the fear of rejection. We're afraid that if we show people the real us—if we let them see our flaws, insecurities, and struggles—they won't accept us. We fear that we'll be judged, dismissed, or pushed away. And so, we build walls to protect ourselves, thinking that if we never let people get too close, we can avoid the pain of rejection.

But here's the paradox: the more we hide, the more disconnected we become. The very thing we're afraid of—rejection—often happens because we're not allowing ourselves to be fully seen. When we guard our hearts, we create distance between ourselves and others, preventing the deep connection we long for.

Connection can only happen when we allow ourselves to be vulnerable. It's in our openness, our authenticity, that others find something real to connect with. Vulnerability is the bridge between isolation and intimacy.

PRACTICAL WISDOM: USING VULNERABILITY TO BUILD DEEPER RELATIONSHIPS

Vulnerability isn't just something to practice in your personal life—it's essential in every area, including work, friendships, and family dynamics. When we allow ourselves to be vulnerable, we create space for others to be vulnerable, too. We develop a culture of empathy and understanding rather than judgment and criticism.

Here are a few ways you can start integrating vulnerability into your relationships:

1. **Be Honest About Your Feelings**: Instead of giving surface-level responses, try being honest about your feelings. For example, if a friend asks how you're doing and you've been feeling overwhelmed, you might say, "I've been struggling a bit lately, but I'm working through it." Vulnerability opens the door to deeper conversations and connections.

2. **Admit When You Don't Have the Answers**: It's okay to admit when you don't know something personally and professionally. Saying, "I'm not sure, but I'm willing to

learn," shows humility and openness. It allows others to see you as human, not as someone who always has to have it all together.

3. **Ask for Help**: Vulnerability often means admitting you can't do it alone. Whether you're feeling overwhelmed with personal responsibilities or facing a challenging project, asking for help is not a sign of weakness—it's an act of courage. It shows that you're willing to trust others and lean on them for support.

4. **Create Space for Others to Be Vulnerable**: Vulnerability is reciprocal. When you open up, you create a safe space for others to do the same. Practice active listening and offer empathy when someone shares their vulnerabilities with you. By creating a culture of openness, you deepen your connections with those around you.

EXERCISE: STRENGTHENING VULNERABILITY IN RELATIONSHIPS

Here's a simple but powerful exercise to help you strengthen your relationships through vulnerability:

1. **Choose a Relationship**: Consider deepening a relationship with a partner, friend, family member, or colleague.

2. **Identify a Moment to Share**: Reflect on a time you held back from being fully vulnerable in this relationship. What stopped you? What were you afraid of sharing?

3. **Plan to Be Open**: Share something authentic and vulnerable in your next interaction. You might say, "I've been meaning to tell you something I've been holding back..." and then express what's on your mind. Remember, vulnerability doesn't have to be perfect—it just has to be honest.

4. **Notice the Connection**: Observe how the other person responds after the conversation. Did it create a deeper connection? Vulnerability often invites more empathy and closeness.

THE SUMMIT OF VULNERABILITY: FINDING STRENGTH IN OPENNESS

Vulnerability is often seen as a risk, but it's one of the most extraordinary acts of courage you can undertake. It requires stepping into the unknown and trusting that your true self is enough. It means showing up fully, even when you don't know how others will respond.

But I've learned that the more you practice vulnerability, the stronger you become. Each time you allow yourself to be seen, you grow. You build deeper relationships, not just with others, but with yourself. And in those moments of openness, you realize that vulnerability is not a weakness—it's the foundation of strength.

The summit of vulnerability is a place of freedom. It's where you stop hiding and start living authentically. It's where you embrace your imperfections, knowing they don't define you. It's where you allow yourself to be accurate; you find your most significant power in that realness.

MEMORABLE QUOTE:

"Vulnerability is the bravest thing you can be. It's the act of showing up fully, even when you're afraid of being seen."

CHAPTER 4: NAVIGATING LIFE'S STORMS

Introduction: Embracing Change and Uncertainty

"Change is the storm that tests our roots. It shakes us, uproots us, and forces us to bend—but it is also what makes us grow."

We've all experienced moments when the winds of change seem overwhelming. Whether it's a career shift, a relationship ending, or a significant life transition, change can feel like a storm that threatens to pull us under. And with change comes fear—the fear of the unknown, the fear of losing control, and the fear that we might be unable to handle what comes next.

I've had my share of life storms, moments when everything felt uncertain and unstable. In those moments, fear was a constant companion. But over time, I learned something valuable: change, though often uncomfortable, is also a catalyst for growth. The storms we face are not meant to destroy us but to transform us.

This chapter will explore navigating life's inevitable storms with resilience and courage. We'll learn to embrace change as an opportunity for growth and gracefully move through uncertainty.

MY STORY: WEATHERING MY STORMS

There was a point in my life when everything felt like falling apart. I was in the middle of a significant career transition, uncertain about my next steps, and faced personal challenges at home. My role as a mental health professional had shifted in unexpected ways, and I no longer felt aligned with the work I was doing. At the same time, I struggled to balance my responsibilities as a mother, and it seemed like every part of my life was in flux.

The fear of not knowing what was coming next was paralyzing. I was terrified that I couldn't handle the changes and would fail both in my career and at home. I felt like I was standing in the middle of a storm, with no clear direction and no idea how to move forward.

But as the weeks turned into months, something shifted. I realized that the storm I was facing wasn't something I could avoid or control—it was something I had to move through. Though uncomfortable, I had to let go of my need for certainty and embrace that change led me toward something new. I began to trust that even though I didn't have all the answers, I had the strength to weather the storm.

Looking back, that transition period was one of my life's most challenging and transformative times. It taught me that we are far more capable than we realize. The storms we face are not meant to break us; they are intended to push us toward growth.

YOUR STORMS: FACING THE FEAR OF CHANGE

Now, I invite you to think about a time when you experienced a significant change. Maybe it was a career shift, the end of a relationship, moving to a new city, or even the uncertainty of pursuing a dream. How did you feel during that time? Did fear show up? Did you resist the change or find a way to move through it?

Change is one of life's constants, yet it's one of the things we fear the most. Change feels so unsettling because it pulls us out of our comfort zone. It forces us to let go of what we know and step into the unknown, where nothing is certain. Uncertainty, for most of us, is deeply uncomfortable.

But here's the truth: change is not something to fear but to embrace. Every time we experience a life storm, we have the opportunity to grow stronger, wiser, and more resilient. The key is not to resist the storm but to learn how to navigate it courageously.

EXERCISE: REFLECTING ON PAST TRANSITIONS

Let's take a moment to reflect on the storms you've weathered in your life. This exercise will help you recognize how you've navigated change in the past and how you can use those experiences to build resilience for future transitions.

1. **Recall a Significant Life Transition**: Think of a time when you experienced a significant change. This could be related to your career, relationships, health, or any other area where things shifted significantly. Write down the details of that experience.

2. **Identify the Fears You Faced**: What fears arose then? Did you fear failure? Rejection? The unknown? Be honest about the emotions you experienced.

3. **Reflect on How You Navigated the Change**: How did you handle the transition? Did you resist the change or find a way to move through it? What helped you stay grounded during that time?

4. **Recognize the Growth**: Consider the growth from that experience. How did you change as a result of navigating that storm? What lessons did you learn? How are you stronger today because of that experience?

This exercise is designed to help you see that you've already weathered storms and have become more assertive on the other side. It's a reminder that you have the resilience to face whatever changes come your way.

THE FEAR OF THE UNKNOWN: LETTING GO OF CONTROL

One of the biggest reasons we fear change is that it diminishes our sense of control. When life is predictable, we feel safe. We know what to expect, and we can plan accordingly. But when change happens—wildly unexpected—we're forced into the unknown, where control slips through our fingers.

For many of us, the unknown feels like a dark void of uncertainty and risk. We fear that if we step into that void, we'll be met with failure, disappointment, or loss. So, we resist change. We cling to the familiar, even when it no longer serves us because at least the familiar feels safe.

But here's the thing: growth doesn't happen in the comfort zone. It occurs in the space of uncertainty. The unknown, while uncomfortable, is also where possibility lives. It's where new opportunities, relationships, and experiences are born.

Letting go of control doesn't mean being reckless or passive. It means trusting that even though you can't predict the outcome, you have the strength and resilience to handle whatever comes your way. It means surrendering to the flow of life and believing that the storm you're facing is guiding you toward something more significant.

PRACTICAL WISDOM: NAVIGATING CHANGE WITH GRACE

Change is inevitable, but how we navigate it is a choice. Here are some practical tools to help you move through life's storms with resilience and grace:

1. **Ground Yourself in the Present**: When we face change, our minds often race ahead, imagining all the worst-case scenarios. To combat this, practice grounding yourself in the present moment. Focus on what you can control right now, and take things one step at a time.

2. **Embrace Flexibility**: One of the greatest strengths you can develop during change is flexibility. Life rarely goes according to plan, and the more adaptable you are, the better equipped you'll be to handle unexpected shifts. Remind yourself that it's okay to adjust your course.

3. **Seek Support**: You don't have to navigate life's storms alone. Contact friends, family, or mentors who can offer guidance and support. Sometimes, just having someone to talk to can make all the difference.

4. **Focus on What's Within Your Control**: When change feels overwhelming, focus on the things you can control—your mindset, actions, and responses. While you can't control the storm, you can control how you move through it.

EXERCISE: LETTING GO OF CONTROL

Here's an exercise to help you practice letting go of control and embracing the uncertainty of life's storms:

1. **Identify an Area Where you resist change**: Think of an area where you resist change. Maybe it's a job you've outgrown, a relationship that no longer feels right, or a decision you've been avoiding because of fear.

2. **Acknowledge the Fear**: What is holding you back from embracing this change? Please write it down. Sometimes, just acknowledging the fear is enough to loosen its grip.

3. **Ask Yourself What You Can Control**: What can you control in this situation? Focus on the actions, decisions, or mindset shifts within your power.

4. **Release the Rest**: Now, consciously let go of the need to control the outcome. Trust that even though you don't know how everything will unfold, you have the strength to handle whatever comes your way.

This exercise is about practicing trust—trusting yourself, trusting the process, and trusting that change, though uncomfortable, is leading you toward growth.

REFLECTION: GROWTH THROUGH LIFE'S STORMS

Life's storms are not something to be feared—they are something to be navigated. Every time you face a period of change, you can grow stronger, deepen your resilience, and become more aligned with who you are.

The storms we face don't just shape us—they reveal us. They show us what we're capable of, what we value, and what we're willing to fight for. We are not the same as before when we come out on the other side. We are more robust, wiser, and more courageous.

As you move through your storms, remember that you've weathered change and will weather it again. Each time you face the unknown, you are building the strength to navigate whatever life brings your way.

MEMORABLE QUOTE:

"The storms we face are not meant to break us. They are meant to awaken the strength we didn't know we had."

CHAPTER 5: FEAR AND FAILURE: REDEFINING SUCCESS

Introduction: The Power of Failure

"Failure is not the opposite of success—it's the foundation. The missteps teach us to walk, and the wrong turns guide us toward our path."

There's a persistent myth that failure is something to avoid, a detour on the road to success. We've been taught to fear failure, to see it as a sign that we're not capable or worthy. But what if failure isn't something to fear at all? What if failure is an essential part of the process, the very thing that leads us to our greatest successes?

I used to fear failure with every fiber of my being. The idea of making a mistake, of falling short, terrified me. I believed that if I failed, it would mean I wasn't good enough. But over time, I realized something profound: failure is not the end of the road. It's part of the journey. Every failure teaches us something invaluable that brings us closer to where we need to be.

In this chapter, we'll explore how to redefine failure, not as something to avoid but as a necessary stepping stone on the path to growth and success. We'll look at how fear of failure holds us back and how we can shift our mindset to embrace failure as a powerful tool for learning and progress.

MY STORY: FAILING FORWARD

I remember early in my career when failure felt like the world's end. I was working on a significant project that could potentially open new doors for me professionally. I poured my heart and soul into it, staying up late, second-guessing every decision, and worrying constantly about how it would be received.

But despite my efforts, the project didn't go as planned. It fell short of expectations, and the feedback I received was far from positive. I was devastated. I remember sitting in my office, feeling like all my hard work had been for nothing. The weight of failure pressed down on me, and I began questioning whether I was cut out for my chosen path.

For weeks, I avoided thinking about the project, too embarrassed to face what I saw as a colossal failure. But then something shifted. I began to look at the feedback I received not as criticism but as guidance. I started to see where I could improve and what I could do differently next time. Slowly, I realized that failure wasn't the end of the road—it was the beginning of a new one.

Though that project didn't succeed in the way I had hoped, it taught me lessons I couldn't have learned any other way. It made me stronger, more resilient, and more determined to grow. It taught me that failure is not something to avoid but something to embrace because the seed of success lies within every failure.

YOUR FEAR OF FAILURE: HOW IT HOLDS YOU BACK

Now, think about your relationship with failure. When you think about pursuing a new goal, taking a risk, or stepping outside your comfort zone, does the fear of failure hold you back? Does the voice in your head whisper, *What if I fail? What if I'm not good enough?*

We all have those fears. Fear of failure is one of the most common fears we face, and it can paralyze us, keeping us stuck in our comfort zones. But here's the thing: staying in your comfort zone might feel safe, but it's not where growth happens. Growth requires risk, and with risk comes the possibility of failure.

But failure is not something to be feared. It's something to be welcomed because every failure brings an opportunity to learn, adjust, and try again. The fear of failure only has power when we let it stop us from moving forward.

EXERCISE: REFRAMING YOUR FEAR OF FAILURE

Here's an exercise to help you reframe your relationship with failure so you can see it as a stepping stone to success rather than something to avoid.

1. **Think of a Goal or Dream You've Been Avoiding**: Start by thinking of a goal or dream you've been putting off because of fear of failure. Maybe it's starting a new business, writing a book, pursuing a promotion, or even trying something new in your personal life.

2. **Identify the Fear of Failure**: What specific fear holds you back? Please write it down. Be honest with yourself. For example:

   - *I'm afraid I'll fail and embarrass myself.*
   - *I'm afraid people will think I'm not good enough.*
   - *I'm afraid I'll waste my time and energy on something that doesn't work.*

3. **Reframe the Fear**: Reframe that fear as an opportunity for growth. Ask yourself:

   - *What would I learn if I failed?*
   - *How could this experience, even if it doesn't go as planned, help me grow?*
   - *What is the worst that could happen, and is it as bad as I'm imagining?*

4. **Take a Small Step Forward**: Take one small step toward that goal, even in fear. It doesn't have to be a big step —just something that moves you toward your dream. You begin to break the fear's hold over you by taking action.

This exercise is about shifting your mindset from avoiding failure to embracing it as part of the journey. The more you practice reframing your fear, the less power it will have over you.

THE GIFT OF FAILURE: WHAT IT TEACHES US

One of the greatest gifts of failure is the lessons it teaches us. When we fail, we can see things from a new perspective, learn what doesn't work, and adjust our approach. Failure is a mirror that reflects areas where we can grow, improve, and become stronger.

Think about some of the most successful people in the world. Do you think they achieved success without ever failing? Of course not. Most successful people will tell you that their failures were essential to their journey. Every failure taught them something valuable—something they couldn't have learned from success alone.

Failure teaches us resilience, perseverance, how to get back up after we've been knocked down, and, most importantly, that we can handle challenges, even when things don't go as planned.

PRACTICAL WISDOM: REDEFINING SUCCESS AND FAILURE

We must redefine what success and failure mean to overcome the fear of failure. Here are some practical ways to start shifting your mindset around failure and success:

1. **Success is Progress, Not Perfection**: Redefine success as progress rather than perfection. Success isn't about getting everything right the first time—it's about making steady progress toward your goals, learning from your mistakes, and continuing to move forward.

2. **Failure is Feedback**: Instead of seeing failure as a negative outcome, start seeing it as feedback. Every time you fail, you're given valuable information about what doesn't work, and that feedback helps you adjust your course. Failure is not a dead end—it's a detour that points you in a new direction.

3. **Celebrate Your Effort**: Focus on celebrating the effort you put into something rather than just the outcome. Even if things don't go as planned, recognize the courage it took to try, the work you put in, and the progress you made. The effort is worth celebrating, regardless of the result.

EXERCISE: REDEFINING SUCCESS AND FAILURE

Let's take a moment to redefine what success and failure mean in your life. This exercise will help you shift your mindset and reduce the power that fear of failure has over you.

1. **Choose a Goal**: Write down a goal you've been working toward or one you've been hesitant to pursue because of fear of failure. It could be something big, like changing careers, or something personal, like building deeper relationships.

2. **Redefine Success**: Now, redefine success to emphasize progress and effort, not perfection. For example:

   - *Success is taking one small step toward this goal every day.*
   - *Success is learning from each mistake and continuing to move forward.*

3. **Reframe Failure**: Next, redefine failure as part of the process. Write down how failure will serve as feedback, not a final judgment. For example:

   - *Failure is a lesson, not a verdict—part of my growth journey.*
   - *Each failure brings me closer to the clarity I need to succeed.*

By redefining success and failure in this way, you begin to see failure not as something to fear but as a necessary part of achieving your goals.

REFLECTION: EMBRACING FAILURE AS A PATH TO GROWTH

Failure is not the enemy. It is often our most excellent teacher. Every time we fail, we are allowed to learn, grow, and become stronger. The key is not to avoid failure but to embrace it as part of the journey toward success.

As you move forward, I encourage you to stop seeing failure as something to fear. Instead, see it as a tool that helps you refine your path, build resilience, and develop the skills you need to succeed. Failure is not the opposite of success; it is the foundation upon which success is built.

The more you embrace failure, the more you will realize that it is not something to be avoided—it is something to be welcomed. Each failure brings you closer to the person you are meant to become.

MEMORABLE QUOTE:

"Failure is not a dead end. It's the road that leads you to your greatest potential."

CHAPTER 6: THE COURAGE TO LET GO

Introduction: The Weight We Carry

"Letting go is not about giving up—it's about giving yourself permission to grow beyond what no longer fits."

There's a moment in everyone's life when we realize we are holding on to something that no longer serves us. It could be a relationship, a friendship, a belief, or even a version of ourselves that we've outgrown. Yet, despite knowing that we need to let go, we cling to it out of fear—fear of change, fear of loss, fear of the unknown.

I've held onto things for far too long in my own life. Whether it was a friendship that had run its course or an old belief no longer aligned with who I was becoming, letting go always felt like a risk. It felt like giving up. But I learned over time that letting go is not about surrendering—it's about making space for something new. It's about trusting that what lies ahead is more aligned with your growth than what you leave behind.

In this chapter, we'll explore the fear that keeps us holding on and how to find the courage to let go when it's time to move forward.

MY STORY: LETTING GO OF A FRIENDSHIP

I had a friend, someone I'd known for years. We met in college and instantly bonded over our shared experiences. We spent late nights talking about life, love, and everything. Our friendship was a source of joy and comfort in my life for a long time. We laughed, cried, and supported each other through tough times.

But as the years went by, something changed. I noticed that our conversations became more one-sided, with me doing most of the listening and her doing most of the talking. Our time together felt draining rather than uplifting, and I often left our hangouts feeling emotionally exhausted. It wasn't that she had done anything wrong—we had grown in different directions. But despite recognizing this, I couldn't bring myself to let go of the friendship.

The thought of ending the friendship felt overwhelming. What if she thought I was abandoning her? What if I was making a mistake? We had shared so much history—how could I walk away from that?

So, I held on, even as the friendship became more of a burden than a joy. I told myself that maybe things would improve and that I needed to be more patient. But deep down, I knew it wasn't right. I knew I was holding on out of fear.

One evening, after yet another emotionally exhausting conversation, I realized I couldn't do it anymore. I couldn't keep pretending that everything was fine when it wasn't. I knew that letting go of the friendship wasn't about abandoning her—it was about choosing to honor where I was in my own life.

With a heavy heart, I had an honest conversation with her. I explained how I felt, how we had grown apart, and how I needed to step back from the friendship for my well-being. It was one of the most challenging conversations I've ever had but also one of the most liberating. For the first time in a long time, I felt like I could breathe again.

Letting go didn't mean erasing our history. It didn't mean I didn't care about her anymore. It simply meant acknowledging that we were no longer on the same path—and that was okay.

YOUR STORY: WHAT ARE YOU HOLDING ON TO?

Now, I invite you to think about your own life. What are you holding onto that no longer serves you? Is it a friendship like mine, where the connection has shifted and no longer feels aligned? Is it a belief about yourself that is keeping you stuck? Or is it a version of yourself you've outgrown but are afraid to let go of because it's all you've known?

We all have things we hold onto out of fear. Fear tells us that if we let go, we'll lose something valuable and be left with nothing. But here's the truth: letting go is not about losing but making space for something new. It's about trusting that you're opening the door to something more aligned with who you are becoming by releasing what no longer fits.

EXERCISE: IDENTIFYING WHAT NO LONGER SERVES YOU

Let's take a moment to reflect on the things in your life that may no longer be serving you. This exercise will help you identify what you're holding onto and why it's time to let go.

1. **Identity What You're Holding Onto**: Think about a relationship, a belief, or a situation that you're holding onto, even though it no longer feels right. Please write it down. Be specific about what it is and why you've been holding onto it.

2. **Acknowledge the Fear**: What keeps you from letting go? Are you afraid of hurting someone's feelings? Are you fearful of stepping into the unknown? Write down the specific fears that are holding you back.

3. **Reflect on How It's Impacting You**: How is holding onto this thing affecting your life? Is it draining your energy? Is it keeping you from growing? Be honest with yourself about the impact it's having on your well-being.

4. **Imagine Letting It Go**: Take a moment to imagine what your life would feel like if you let go of this thing. How would you feel if you no longer carried this

weight? What new opportunities might open up if you made space for something new?

This exercise clarifies what's holding you back and why it's time to let go. Letting go isn't easy, but it's often the first step toward making space for growth.

THE FEAR OF LETTING GO: WHY WE HOLD ON

The fear of letting go is deeply rooted in the fear of loss. We hold on because we're afraid that we'll lose something irreplaceable if we let go. We're so scared of the void that might be left behind, of the uncertainty that comes with stepping into the unknown.

But here's the truth: holding on to something that no longer serves you is far more draining than letting go. When we cling to things out of fear, we prevent ourselves from growing. We keep ourselves stuck in a place that no longer feels right, all because we're afraid of what might happen if we release our grip.

Letting go isn't about giving up—it's about trusting that what's ahead is more aligned with who you are becoming than what you're leaving behind. It's about recognizing that growth requires space, and sometimes that means releasing the things that are no longer fit.

PRACTICAL WISDOM: FINDING THE COURAGE TO LET GO

Letting go is one of the hardest things we can do, but it's also one of the most important. Here are some practical steps to help you find the courage to let go of what no longer serves you:

1. **Honor the Past**: Before you let go, take a moment to honor what that relationship, belief, or situation brought into your life. Acknowledge the lessons you learned, the growth you experienced, and the memories you made. Letting go doesn't mean erasing the past—it means making peace with it.

2. **Trust Yourself**: You know what's best for you. If something no longer feels right, trust that it's okay to move on. You are the expert in your life, and only you can decide what aligns with your growth.

3. **Create Space for Grief**: Letting go often comes with a sense of grief, even if you know it's the right thing to do. Allow yourself to grieve the loss of what once was, but don't let that grief keep you stuck. It's okay to feel sadness but remember that letting go is also a form of self-care.

4. **Focus on What's Ahead**: When you let go of something that no longer serves you, you create space for something new to enter your life. Focus on the possibilities that await you once you release the old.

What new opportunities, relationships, or experiences might be on the horizon?

EXERCISE: LETTING GO WITH INTENTION

Here's an exercise to help you practice letting go with intention:

1. **Write a Letter**: Write a letter to the person, belief, or situation you're letting go of. In the letter, express gratitude for what it brought into your life and acknowledge the lessons you learned. Then, gently release it by writing, *"I am letting you go now, with love and gratitude."* You don't need to send a letter—it's for you.

2. **Create a Ritual of Release**: Once you've written your letter, create a ritual to symbolize letting go. You might burn the letter, tear it up, or bury it. Choose a method that feels meaningful to you. The act of physically releasing the letter can help solidify the emotional release.

3. **Set an Intention for What's Next**: After letting go, set an intention for what you want to invite into your life. Write down what you're making space for—whether it's new friendships, opportunities, or personal growth. Keep this intention close as a reminder of your new path.

This exercise is about honoring what you're letting go of while creating space for what's to come. Letting go is an act of courage, paving the way for new possibilities and growth.

EMBRACING CHANGE: THE FREEDOM IN LETTING GO

Letting go is not just about removing something from your life —it's about freeing yourself from the weight of what no longer serves you. When we hold on too tightly to people, beliefs, or situations that no longer align with who we are, we limit our ability to grow into the person we are meant to become. Letting go is an act of self-liberation, a declaration that you are ready to move forward and embrace the next chapter of your life.

I remember feeling a mix of emotions after I let go of that long-standing friendship—grief, relief, and a sense of freedom. It wasn't easy, and there were moments when I doubted my decision. But over time, I began to feel lighter. I started reconnecting with other friends who lifted me, friends who supported the person I was becoming. I made space for new relationships aligned with my values and growth.

Letting go created room for me to grow, allowing me to explore new possibilities that I hadn't even considered while I was holding onto something that no longer fit. Releasing is a powerful affirmation that you trust yourself and believe you are worthy of the new opportunities that await you.

EXERCISE: EMBRACING THE FREEDOM OF LETTING GO

Here's an exercise to help you fully embrace the freedom of letting go and opening yourself to new possibilities.

1. **Visualize Your Future**: Take a few minutes to close your eyes and visualize your life if you let go of what's no longer serving you. Imagine yourself without the weight of that relationship, belief, or situation. What do you see? How do you feel? Allow yourself to experience the freedom that comes with letting go.

2. **Set a New Intention**: Now that you've created space, set a clear intention for what you want to invite into that space. Be specific about your calling—new friendships, opportunities, personal growth, or inner peace. Please write it down as a reminder of the new path you're stepping into.

3. **Take Action**: Take one small action toward your new intention. It could be reaching out to a new friend, saying yes to an opportunity you've been hesitant about, or reflecting on your growth. By taking action, you're signaling to yourself that you're ready to move forward and embrace the next chapter.

This exercise helps you connect with the sense of freedom from letting go. It reminds you that releasing what no longer serves you creates space for things genuinely aligned with your growth.

REFLECTION: THE COURAGE TO MOVE FORWARD

Letting go is one of the most courageous acts we can do. It acknowledges that we trust ourselves enough to release what no longer serves us and believe in the possibilities. The courage to let go is not about erasing the past but honoring the past while making space for the future.

As you move through your journey of letting go, remember that it's okay to feel a range of emotions—grief, relief, sadness, and joy. Letting go is a process, and it requires both strength and vulnerability. But on the other side of that release is freedom. It's the freedom to grow, explore, and create a life aligned with your authentic self.

The courage to let go is a gift you give yourself. It's the act of saying *I deserve to move forward. I deserve to create space for what truly aligns with me.* And in that space, you'll find the freedom to grow into the person you are meant to be.

MEMORABLE QUOTE:

"Letting go is not the end. It's the beginning of something new that aligns with the person you are becoming."

CHAPTER 7: THE FEAR OF VULNERABILITY IN RELATIONSHIPS

Introduction: The Walls We Build

"Vulnerability is the gateway to true intimacy, but it requires the courage to be seen, to risk rejection, and to open our hearts."

Relationships are where we feel the most joy and connection and where our deepest fears often emerge. Fear of rejection, abandonment, and vulnerability can all create barriers between us and the people we care about. We build walls around our hearts to protect ourselves, thinking that if we hide the parts of us that feel too tender or insecure, we'll stay safe. But those walls also isolate us, preventing us from experiencing the fullness of connection and love that relationships offer.

For most of my life, I struggled with vulnerability in relationships. If I let someone see the real me—my fears, insecurities, and flaws—they might pull away. I thought that being vulnerable was too risky, too dangerous. But over time, I learned that vulnerability is not a weakness—it is the very thing that strengthens relationships. Through vulnerability, we create the deep, meaningful connections we crave.

In this chapter, we will explore the fear of vulnerability in relationships and how embracing that fear can lead to more robust, more authentic connections with the people we love.

MY STORY: BREAKING DOWN THE WALLS IN A RELATIONSHIP

I'll never forget when I realized I had been keeping someone I loved at arm's length. It was early in a new relationship, and everything was going well. We had fun together, we laughed, and on the surface, things looked perfect. But beneath the surface, I was holding back. Every time he tried to get closer emotionally, I would retreat. I kept our conversations light, avoiding anything that felt too intimate or revealing. I told myself it was because I wanted to take things slow, but the truth was, I was afraid.

I was afraid that he would lose interest if he saw the real me—the parts of me that were still healing from past hurts, the parts of me that weren't perfect. I had built a wall around my heart, thinking it would protect me from being hurt again. But in doing so, I was also preventing myself from fully experiencing the love and connection that this relationship had the potential to offer.

One evening, after yet another surface-level conversation, he looked at me with concern and said, *"I feel like you're not letting me in. What are you afraid of?"* His question caught me off guard, but at that moment, I realized he was right. I had been so focused on protecting myself that I hadn't allowed myself to be fully open with him. I hadn't given him the chance to see me truly.

With my heart racing, I took a deep breath and decided to share something vulnerable. I told him about my fear of being hurt again, how past relationships had left me guarded, and how scared I was to open up fully. I expected him to pull away, to tell me that I was too much or that my fears were unfounded. But instead, he listened. He just listened and didn't judge me or try to fix anything.

At that moment, something shifted. The wall I had built around my heart began to crumble, and for the first time, I felt indeed seen. It was terrifying, but it was also liberating. Allowing myself to be vulnerable created a space for deeper connection and understanding. The relationship grew stronger, not because I was perfect, but because I was honest.

YOUR STORY: WHERE ARE YOU HOLDING BACK?

Now, think about your relationships. Where are you holding back? Is there a part of yourself you're afraid to share with your partner, friend, or even a family member? Are there conversations you're avoiding because they feel too vulnerable or too risky?

We all have areas in our relationships where we hold back out of fear. Maybe it's the fear of being rejected, the fear of not being enough, or the fear of showing someone our true selves. But here's the truth: vulnerability is the foundation of intimacy. It allows us to connect with another person profoundly and meaningfully truly. Without vulnerability, relationships remain surface-level, and we miss out on the richness of emotional connection.

EXERCISE: OPENING UP IN RELATIONSHIPS

Let's take a moment to reflect on how you can begin to open up more in your relationships. This exercise will help you identify where you're holding back and how to embrace vulnerability safely and in a supportive way.

1. **Identify a Relationship Where You're Holding Back**: Think about one relationship where you feel you're holding back emotionally. This could be with a partner, a close friend, or a family member. Write down the person's name and how you're not fully showing up in the relationship.

2. **Acknowledge the Fear**: What specific fear holds you back in this relationship? Are you afraid of being judged? Are you scared of being rejected or misunderstood? Be honest with yourself about the fear keeping you from being fully vulnerable.

3. **Start Small**: Vulnerability doesn't mean sharing everything simultaneously. It's about starting small and opening up little by little. Think of a tiny thing you can share with this person that feels vulnerable but manageable. It could be sharing a personal fear, admitting a mistake, or expressing something you've held back.

4. **Observe the Response**: Observe how the person responds once you've shared. Did they offer empathy? Did they listen without judgment? When we allow

ourselves to be vulnerable, we create a space for deeper connection, and the other responds with care and understanding.

5. **Reflect on How It Felt**: After the conversation, take a moment to reflect on how it felt to open up. Did it strengthen your connection with the person? Did you feel more seen, understood, and connected?

This exercise is about practicing vulnerability safely and gradually. The more you open up, the more you see that vulnerability leads to deeper, more authentic connections.

THE FEAR OF REJECTION: WHY WE PROTECT OURSELVES

One of the biggest reasons we avoid vulnerability in relationships is the fear of rejection. We worry that if we show someone our true selves—our flaws, insecurities, and fears—they might not accept us. If we hide those parts of ourselves, we'll be safer, lovable, and accepted. But in reality, hiding only keeps us disconnected.

The fear of rejection is deeply ingrained in our need for connection and belonging. We all want to be loved and accepted for who we are, but the irony is that we can't truly experience that love and acceptance if we're not showing up authentically. True intimacy requires risk. It requires us to let go of the need for perfection and to trust that we are enough, even with our imperfections.

PRACTICAL WISDOM: EMBRACING VULNERABILITY IN RELATIONSHIPS

Vulnerability is a practice, not a one-time event. It requires continuous courage to show up as your true self in relationships. Here are some practical ways to start embracing vulnerability in your relationships:

1. **Be Honest About Your Emotions**: Instead of brushing off your feelings or pretending everything is fine, practice being honest about what's happening inside. If you're feeling hurt, anxious, or uncertain, express that to the person you're close to. Vulnerability begins with emotional honesty.

2. **Admit When You're Wrong**: Vulnerability also means owning up to your mistakes. If you've hurt someone or made a misstep, be willing to apologize and take responsibility. Admitting when you're wrong shows humility and strengthens trust in relationships.

3. **Ask for What You Need**: Many people are afraid to ask for what they need in relationships because they don't want to appear needy or burdensome. But asking for emotional support, reassurance, or even space when required is a sign of strength, not weakness. It shows that you value the relationship enough to be clear

about your needs.

4. **Hold Space for Others**: Vulnerability is a two-way street. When someone you care about opens up to you, practice holding space for them. Listen without judgment, offer empathy, and resist the urge to fix their problems. By creating a safe space for vulnerability, you deepen the connection in the relationship.

EXERCISE: PRACTICING VULNERABILITY WITH EMPATHY

Here's an exercise to help you practice vulnerability while also creating space for others to be vulnerable in your relationships:

1. **Choose a Relationship to Deepen**: Think of one relationship in your life where you'd like to deepen the connection through vulnerability. This could be with a partner, a close friend, or a family member.

2. **Start by Sharing Something Personal**: In your following conversation with this person, share something that feels vulnerable but safe. It could be a fear you've been carrying, an insecurity you're dealing with, or an experience that shaped you.

3. **Invite Them to Share**: After you've opened up, invite the other person to share something. You might say, *"I'd love to hear how you feel about this too."* By creating a space for mutual vulnerability, you invite deeper connections.

Offer Empathy and Understanding: Practice listening without judgment when the other person shares. Offer empathy and resist the urge to offer solutions unless they ask for them. Sometimes, the greatest gift we can offer someone is simply being present and listening with empathy.

5. **Reflect Together**: After both of you have shared, take a moment to reflect on how it felt to open up. Did it bring you closer? Did you think of a more profound sense of understanding and connection? Discuss how being vulnerable with each other strengthened the bond between you.

This exercise helps create a cycle of mutual vulnerability, where both people feel safe to open up and be authentic. Through this practice, relationships grow more robust, intimate, and resilient.

THE POWER OF VULNERABILITY: STRENGTHENING RELATIONSHIPS THROUGH OPENNESS

Vulnerability is often viewed as a risk but is a powerful tool for deepening relationships. When we allow ourselves to be seen fully—flaws, insecurities, and all—we give the people in our lives the opportunity to love us for who we are. Vulnerability removes our masks and allows us to connect on a deeper, more meaningful level.

One of the most beautiful aspects of vulnerability is that it creates space for trust to grow. When you open up to someone, you say, *"I trust you enough to show you my true self."* And when that trust is reciprocated, it forms the foundation of a relationship built on authenticity and mutual respect.

In my experience, the relationships that have flourished the most are where I've been willing to be vulnerable. Whether sharing a personal fear, admitting when I didn't have it all together, or expressing my needs honestly, vulnerability created a pathway to deeper intimacy and connection. It allowed me to let go of the fear of rejection and trust that I could be loved just as I am.

EXERCISE: BUILDING TRUST THROUGH VULNERABILITY

Here's a simple but powerful exercise to help you build trust through vulnerability in your relationships:

1. **Choose One Relationship to Focus On.** Think of a relationship where you want to build more trust and openness. This could be a romantic partner, a friend, or a family member.

2. **Share Something Real**: The next time you're with this person, share something that feels honest and real. It doesn't have to be something big—it could be as simple as saying, *"I've been feeling a little insecure about something lately, and I wanted to talk about it."* The key is to be genuine and open.

3. **Ask for Their Perspective**: After you've shared, ask for their thoughts or feelings on the topic. This invites the other person to open up, creating a space for mutual vulnerability.

4. **Acknowledge Their Openness**: When the other person shares with you, acknowledge their vulnerability and express appreciation for their openness. You might say, *"Thank you for sharing that with me—I appreciate your honesty."*

5. **Notice the Trust Building**: As you practice vulnerability and openness, notice how the trust

between you and the other person grows over time. Trust isn't built in one moment—it's built over time through consistent acts of vulnerability and understanding.

This exercise encourages mutual trust and vulnerability, creating a safe space where both people feel comfortable being authentic. It's through this openness that relationships are indeed strengthened.

REFLECTION: THE COURAGE TO BE VULNERABLE IN LOVE AND FRIENDSHIP

Vulnerability is the bridge between surface-level relationships and deep, meaningful connections. It's the courage to show up fully, to risk rejection, and to trust that you are worthy of love just as you are. In love, friendship, and family relationships, vulnerability is the key that unlocks true intimacy.

As you reflect on your relationships, ask yourself: *Where can I be more vulnerable? Where can I show up more authentically?* Vulnerability is not about perfection—it's about being authentic. It's about letting go of the need to be flawless and embracing the beauty of being human.

The more you practice vulnerability, the more you will experience the richness of connection that comes with it. You will find that the relationships in your life grow more robust, resilient, and fulfilling when you allow yourself to be seen and accepted for who you are.

MEMORABLE QUOTE:

"True intimacy is built on vulnerability. It's the courage to show up fully, to be seen, and to trust that you are worthy of love just as you are.

CHAPTER 8: FEAR OF ABANDONMENT AND THE POWER OF SELF-LOVE

Introduction: The Shadow of Abandonment

"The fear of abandonment is a shadow that follows us in relationships, whispering that we are not enough. But when we learn to love ourselves fully, that shadow fades."

The fear of abandonment is one of the most common and deeply rooted fears we face in relationships. It stems from the belief that if we let someone get too close, they will eventually leave us, and we will be left alone, rejected, and unloved. This overwhelming fear can lead us to cling too tightly to others or push them away before they can leave us. It's a fear that many of us don't like to admit we have, yet it shows up in subtle and not-so-subtle ways in our relationships.

I've felt the grip of this fear many times in my life. I didn't realize how much it affected my relationships for years. I could prevent people from leaving me if I worked hard enough to be the "perfect" partner, friend, or family member. But in doing so, I lost touch with myself. I based my worth on how others saw me, which deepened my fear of abandonment.

What I've learned is that the fear of abandonment isn't something that others can fix—it's something that can only be healed from within. The more I cultivated self-love and learned to value myself, the less power that fear had over me. When we truly love ourselves, we realize we are enough, regardless of who stays or leaves. We stop seeking validation from others and start finding it within ourselves.

MY STORY: CLINGING OUT OF FEAR

There was a time when I clung to a relationship out of fear. I was in a romantic relationship with someone I cared about deeply, but underneath the surface, I was terrified that he would leave me. Whenever he was distant or didn't respond to a message immediately, I thought of rejection. I told myself that if I weren't "good enough," he would walk away if I didn't always make him happy.

I started overcompensating, always trying to anticipate his needs and never wanting to rock the boat. I was constantly worried that something I said or did would push him away. In truth, I wasn't being myself—I was playing a role, hoping that by being the "perfect" partner, I could prevent abandonment.

But the harder I tried, the more distant he seemed to become. No matter how much I gave, it never felt like enough. And the more I clung to him, the more I lost sight of myself. I wasn't just afraid of losing him—I was scared of being alone, of being unloved, of not being enough.

Eventually, the relationship ended, and though the breakup was painful, it taught me one of the most important lessons of my life: I cannot rely on someone else to make me feel worthy. The fear of abandonment wasn't about him leaving me—it was about me not feeling secure in who I was. I realized that until I learned to love myself fully, I would keep repeating the same relationship patterns.

YOUR FEAR OF ABANDONMENT: WHERE DOES IT SHOW UP?

Now, I invite you to think about your own life. Where does the fear of abandonment show up in your relationships? Do you find yourself clinging too tightly to people, afraid they'll leave if you let go? Or do you push people away, afraid that getting too close will only lead to hurt?

Fear of abandonment often manifests in two ways: either we become overly attached and clingy, seeking constant reassurance from others, or we avoid intimacy altogether, keeping people at a distance to protect ourselves from the pain of being left. Both responses stem from the same core belief: *I am not enough.*

But here's the truth: You are enough, just as you are. The fear of abandonment is rooted in a false narrative that you need someone else to complete you, to make you worthy. The more you learn to love and value yourself, the less power this fear will have over you.

EXERCISE: IDENTIFYING AND RELEASING THE FEAR OF ABANDONMENT

Let's explore where the fear of abandonment might be showing up in your life and how you can begin to release it through the power of self-love.

1. **Identify Where the Fear Shows Up**: Consider a relationship where you've noticed the fear of abandonment. Do you find yourself clinging to this person, seeking reassurance or worrying that they will leave? Or do you keep them at arm's length, afraid of getting too close? Write down what you notice.

2. **Acknowledge the Underlying Belief**: What is the underlying belief that's driving this fear? Is it the belief that you're not enough? Do you need to be perfect to be loved? Write down the specific thoughts or beliefs when you think about this fear.

3. **Challenge the Belief**: Now, challenge that belief. Is it true that you need someone else to make you feel worthy? Is it true that you're not enough just as you are? Write down a new belief that supports your inherent worth. For example: *"I am enough, and my worth is not dependent on others."*

4. **Practice Self-Love**: Each day, practice self-love. This could be something as simple as speaking kindly to yourself, setting a boundary, or taking time to do something that nourishes your soul. The more you cultivate self-love, the less you will seek validation from others.

This exercise is about identifying the root of your fear and replacing it with a foundation of self-love. When you love yourself fully, the fear of abandonment begins to lose grip.

THE POWER OF SELF-LOVE: HEALING THE FEAR OF ABANDONMENT

Self-love is the antidote to the fear of abandonment. We no longer need to cling to others for validation or security when we love ourselves. We stop fearing that someone will leave us because we know our worth isn't tied to whether someone stays or goes.

Self-love doesn't happen overnight—it's a daily practice of showing up for yourself and treating yourself with the same kindness, compassion, and care you would offer someone you love. It's about recognizing that you are whole and complete, just as you are, and that no one else can fill the void inside of you.

When I began practicing self-love, I noticed a profound relationship shift. I no longer sought constant reassurance from others because I knew I was enough. I stopped fearing that people would leave me because I realized that my happiness didn't depend on them. The more I loved myself, the more I attracted healthy, balanced, and fulfilling relationships.

PRACTICAL WISDOM: CULTIVATING SELF-LOVE IN RELATIONSHIPS

Here are some practical steps to help you cultivate self-love in your relationships and release the fear of abandonment:

1. **Set Healthy Boundaries**: Self-love means honoring your needs and setting boundaries when necessary. In relationships, this might mean saying no when you need space, asking for time to focus on yourself, or being clear about what you need to feel secure. Boundaries are not a sign of distance—they are a sign of respect for yourself and others.

2. **Reassure yourself**: Instead of seeking constant reassurance from others, practice giving it to yourself. When insecurity or fear arises, remind yourself that you are enough and that your worth is not dependent on anyone else. Speak to yourself with kindness and compassion, just as you would to a dear friend.

3. **Spend Time Alone**: One of the best ways to cultivate self-love is by spending quality time with yourself. Whether going for a walk, journaling, meditating, or simply doing something you enjoy, being alone allows you to reconnect with your inner self and strengthen your sense of worth.

4. **Release the Need for Perfection**: The fear of abandonment is often tied to the belief that we must be perfect to be loved. But love isn't about perfection—it's about authenticity. The more you allow yourself to be imperfect, the more you'll see that you are worthy of love just as you are.

EXERCISE: PRACTICING SELF-LOVE AND RELEASING THE FEAR

Here's an exercise to help you practice self-love and release the fear of abandonment in your relationships:

1. **Write a Love Letter to Yourself**: Write a letter to yourself as if you were writing to someone you love deeply. In the letter, express gratitude for who you are, acknowledge your strengths, and remind yourself that you are enough. This letter is a way to affirm your worth and build a foundation of self-love.

2. **Release the Fear in a Ritual**: Once you've written your love letter, create a ritual to symbolize releasing the fear of abandonment. You might write down your worries on a piece of paper and then burn it or tear it up as a way of letting go. As you do this, say aloud, *"I release the fear of abandonment and embrace my worth."*

1. **Celebrate Your Worth**: After completing the ritual, do something that celebrates your worth and brings you joy. Whether treating yourself to a special meal, spending time in nature, or simply relaxing with a good book, take time to honor yourself and the love you are cultivating.

This exercise is about letting go of the fear of abandonment and stepping into the power of self-love. The more you practice loving yourself, the more you realize you are enough, and the fear of abandonment will fade.

REFLECTION: EMBRACING SELF-LOVE AND LETTING GO OF FEAR

The fear of abandonment can feel overwhelming, but it doesn't have to control your relationships. When you cultivate self-love, you release the need to seek validation from others. You no longer fear being left or rejected because you know your worth is not dependent on anyone else. You are enough.

As you continue to embrace self-love, you will find that your relationships become healthier, more balanced, and more fulfilling. You will attract people who honor and respect you because you honor and respect yourself. The more you love yourself, the less power the fear of abandonment will have over you.

MEMORABLE QUOTE:

"When you love yourself fully, the fear of abandonment fades, and you realize you are enough—just as you are."

CHAPTER 9: FACING THE FEAR OF CONFLICT IN RELATIONSHIPS

Introduction: The Fear of Disagreement

"Conflict is not the enemy of connection—avoiding it is. We truly understand and grow with each other through honest, open dialogue."

Most of us have experienced the fear of conflict in relationships. Whether with a partner, a friend, or a family member, disagreeing with someone we care about can feel overwhelming. We worry that bringing up an issue will lead to tension, rejection, or even the end of the relationship. Many choose to stay silent, suppress their feelings, and prioritize keeping the peace to avoid these uncomfortable possibilities.

But avoiding conflict doesn't eliminate it—it only pushes it beneath the surface, where it festers and grows. Over time, the unresolved tension can create distance between people, preventing them from truly connecting and understanding each other. Healthy relationships aren't free from conflict; they're strengthened by how we handle disagreements with empathy and open communication.

The key is not to fear conflict but to approach it with the intention of growth, resolution, and mutual respect. Conflict can be a powerful tool for deepening relationships when navigated thoughtfully. In this chapter, we will explore how fear of conflict manifests in relationships and how we can embrace it as an opportunity to strengthen our bonds.

MY STORY: THE SILENT RESENTMENT IN A FRIENDSHIP

I'll never forget how a simple misunderstanding almost cost me one of my most cherished friendships. For years, I had a close friend whom I adored. We shared everything—our hopes, dreams, and challenges. But there was one aspect of our friendship that I kept buried for fear of causing conflict.

She had a habit of canceling plans at the last minute or changing them without much notice, leaving me feeling frustrated and unimportant. Each time it happened, I told myself it wasn't worth mentioning. I didn't want to make a big deal out of it, and I didn't want to hurt her feelings or seem demanding. So, I stayed silent, convincing myself that flexibility was better than creating tension.

But the more I stayed silent, the more resentment built up. I started to feel taken for granted. I agreed to plan out of obligation, but I was hurt underneath the surface. Once filled with joy and excitement, the relationship felt like an emotional weight. And yet, I still avoided the conversation because the fear of conflict loomed.

One evening, after yet another canceled plan, something inside me snapped. I realized that by avoiding conflict, I was not only hurting myself but also damaging the friendship. I wasn't being honest about my needs, and that dishonesty was creating distance. I knew that if I wanted the friendship to survive, I had to have the difficult conversation I had been avoiding.

I called my friend with a pounding heart and gently expressed how I felt. I told her I valued our friendship profoundly but that the frequent cancellations made me feel unimportant. I expected defensiveness or anger, but instead, she was surprised. She hadn't realized how much it had affected me because I had never spoken up. We talked it through, and to my relief, she understood. She apologized and made an effort to be more considerate in the future.

That conversation not only saved our friendship but also deepened it. By addressing the issue, we created space for mutual understanding and respect. It was a turning point that taught me a valuable lesson: avoiding conflict doesn't protect relationships—it prevents them from growing.

YOUR FEAR OF CONFLICT: WHERE ARE YOU HOLDING BACK?

Think about your relationships. Where are you holding back from addressing an issue because you fear conflict? Is there a conversation you've been avoiding because you worry it might cause tension or discomfort? Maybe it's a minor annoyance building over time or a more profound issue you're afraid to bring to the surface.

Conflict is often viewed as a threat to relationships, but it's essential to building trust and intimacy. Avoiding conflict prevents the other person from truly understanding our needs and creates barriers to deeper connection. Relationships thrive on open communication, even when that communication involves difficult conversations.

But how do we move past the fear of conflict? The first step is recognizing that when handled with empathy and care, conflict is not something to fear but to embrace. It's a chance to be honest about our feelings, to listen to the other person's perspective, and to work together toward a resolution that strengthens the relationship.

EXERCISE: PREPARING FOR HEALTHY CONFLICT

Let's dive into an exercise that will help you prepare for and approach conflict healthfully and constructively. This exercise will guide you through identifying the issue, clarifying your needs, and engaging in a meaningful conversation that leads to resolution.

1. **Identify the Issue**: Start by identifying a specific issue in one of your relationships where you've been avoiding conflict. It could be a recurring pattern of behavior that frustrates you, an unresolved disagreement, or something you've been holding back out of fear of upsetting the other person. Please write down the issue and how it affects your feelings toward the relationship.

2. **Reflect on Your Needs**: Before approaching the conversation, take some time to reflect on what you need from the other person and the relationship. Are you seeking more respect, consideration, or understanding? What specific changes would help you feel more comfortable and connected? Be clear with yourself about what you need to communicate effectively.

3. **Consider the Other Person's Perspective**: Conflict is a two-way street, and it's essential to approach the

conversation with empathy. Put yourself in the other person's shoes. What might they be feeling? Are they aware of how their actions are affecting you, or could this come as a surprise to them? Reflecting on their perspective can help you approach the conversation with compassion rather than blame.

4. **Plan Your Approach**: When you're ready to address the issue, plan how to approach the conversation. Start by expressing your feelings using "I" statements rather than blaming or accusing. For example, instead of saying, *"You never respect my time,"* you could say, *"I've been hurt when our plans change at the last minute, and I'd like to talk about how we can make it work for both of us."* This sets the tone for a collaborative conversation rather than a confrontation.

5. **Be Open to Listening**: After you've expressed your feelings, be open to hearing the other person's perspective. They may have a different experience or be unaware of how their actions impact you. Listen with empathy, without interrupting or defending yourself. Actual resolution happens when both sides feel heard and understood.

6. **Work Toward a Solution**: Once you have shared your thoughts and feelings, work together to find a solution that respects your needs. This might involve setting new boundaries, agreeing on different communication methods, or compromising. The goal is to come away from the conversation with a sense of mutual respect and a plan for moving forward.

This exercise helps you approach conflict with intention, empathy, and clarity, ensuring that the conversation leads to deeper understanding rather than increased tension.

THE FEAR OF BEING MISUNDERSTOOD: WHY WE AVOID CONFLICT

One of the most common fears around conflict is being misunderstood. We worry that if we speak up, the other person won't understand our intentions or take our words wrongfully. This fear often leads to silence, even when something is bothering us. But when we avoid expressing our feelings out of fear of being misunderstood, we deny the other person the opportunity to know us honestly.

Being misunderstood can feel isolating, but it's important to remember that communication is a skill, and like any skill, it improves with practice. The more we engage in open, honest conversations—even when uncomfortable—the better we express our needs clearly and understand others. It's okay if not every conversation goes perfectly. What matters is that you're showing up to be authentic and to work through issues together.

In my experience, the fear of being misunderstood is often worse than the reality. I'm usually met with understanding when I approach difficult conversations with honesty and empathy. Even when there's been a misunderstanding, the conversation has opened the door to deeper dialogue and connection.

PRACTICAL WISDOM: EMBRACING CONFLICT AS A PATH TO GROWTH

Conflict can be uncomfortable, but it's also one of the most critical opportunities for growth in relationships. Here are some practical ways to embrace conflict as a path to deeper connection and mutual understanding:

1. **Shift Your Mindset About Conflict**: Instead of viewing conflict as something to avoid, start seeing it as a tool for growth. Conflict doesn't mean something is wrong with the relationship—it means there's an opportunity to deepen understanding. When you shift your mindset, conflict becomes less intimidating and more constructive.

2. **Practice Active Listening**: One of the most powerful skills in navigating conflict is active listening. When the other person is speaking, focus entirely on what they're saying without planning your response or interrupting. Reflect on what you've heard to ensure you're understanding them correctly. This helps prevent misunderstandings and shows that you value their perspective.

3. **Own Your Part in the Conflict**: In any disagreement, both parties play a role. Be willing to acknowledge

your part in the conflict and take responsibility for how your actions may have contributed. This doesn't mean blaming yourself—it means being accountable and open to personal growth.

4. **Keep the Bigger Picture in Mind**: During a conflict, it's easy to get caught up in the details of the argument. But try to keep the bigger picture in mind: the relationship itself. *What's more important —being right or strengthening our connection?* Focusing on the relationship's health rather than winning the argument can help guide you toward a resolution.

5. **Be Patient with the Process**: Conflict resolution isn't always immediate. Sometimes, working through an issue entirely takes multiple conversations or time. Be patient with the process and with each other. The goal is to build understanding and trust, which often happens gradually.

EXERCISE: DEEPENING CONNECTION THROUGH CONFLICT

Here's an exercise designed to help you embrace conflict as a path to deeper connection and growth in your relationships:

1. **Choose a Relationship to Focus On.** Think of a relationship in your life with ongoing tension or unresolved conflict. This could be with a romantic partner, a close friend, or a family member.

2. **Reflect on the Issue**: Reflect on the issue causing tension. Write down how the conflict has affected you emotionally, and consider how avoiding it has impacted the relationship.

3. **Engage in an Honest Conversation**: Set aside time for a calm, thoughtful conversation with the other person. Use the strategies we've discussed—express your feelings using "I" statements, listen actively, and work toward a solution together.

4. **Follow-Up and Check-In**: After the conversation, follow up with the person to check how things are going. Conflict resolution is ongoing, and staying connected and communicating is essential. Ask how they're feeling and share how the resolution has impacted you.

5. **Celebrate the Growth**: Finally, take time to celebrate the growth from the conflict. Whether it's a more

profound understanding, a new boundary set, or simply a feeling of relief from addressing the issue, recognize that conflict has led to positive change.

This exercise helps transform conflict from anxiety into a source of connection and growth. By approaching conflict with openness, empathy, and a focus on resolution, you can strengthen the bonds in your relationships.

REFLECTION: THE POWER OF EMBRACING CONFLICT

Conflict is inevitable, but it doesn't have to be something we fear or avoid. When we approach conflict with empathy, honesty, and a commitment to resolution, it becomes an opportunity for growth and deeper connection. The more we embrace conflict as a natural and necessary part of relationships, the more resilient and fulfilling those relationships will become.

As you progress in your relationships, I encourage you to see conflict not as a threat but as a tool for deepening your understanding of each other. Speak your truth, listen with compassion, and remember that every disagreement is an opportunity to build a stronger, more authentic connection.

MEMORABLE QUOTE:

"True connection isn't the absence of conflict—it's the ability to navigate it with empathy, honesty, and love.

CHAPTER 10: THE FEAR OF INTIMACY AND THE PATH TO DEEPER LOVE

Introduction: The Walls We Build Around Our Hearts

"True intimacy begins where fear ends—when we are willing to be seen, not just as we wish to be, but as we truly are."

We all crave intimacy in relationships, which can also evoke deep fear. The closer we get to someone, the more we risk being vulnerable, exposed, and possibly hurt. Many have experienced moments when we pulled away just as relationships began to deepen—not because we didn't care, but because the fear of being seen felt too overwhelming.

Intimacy requires us to lower our defenses and let someone into the parts of ourselves that we often keep hidden. It's more than just physical closeness; it's emotional and psychological vulnerability. The fear of intimacy isn't just the fear of rejection —it's the fear of being loved and perhaps not living up to the love we receive.

Over the years, I've learned that the fear of intimacy is often rooted in a fear of not being enough. We worry that if someone sees who we are—our flaws, fears, and insecurities—they will pull away. But what if the opposite is true? What if the path to deeper, more fulfilling relationships begins with allowing ourselves to be fully seen, loved, and accepted, imperfections and all?

This chapter will explore the fear of intimacy, how it holds us back in relationships, and how we can embrace vulnerability as the key to experiencing more profound love and connection.

MY STORY: THE FEAR OF BEING TRULY SEEN

I remember a time in my life when I was afraid of intimacy, though I didn't recognize it as fear at the time. I had always believed that I was open to love and wanted deep connections with others. But looking back, I can see that I often kept people at a distance, even in romantic relationships, out of fear that if they saw the real me, they wouldn't stay.

One relationship stands out in particular. We had been dating for a few months, and everything seemed to be going well. We spent time together, laughed, and enjoyed each other's company. But as the relationship grew more serious, I began to pull back. I found reasons to keep my emotional distance. I would deflect when he asked more profound questions, change the subject when things got too personal, and avoid any conversations about the future.

It wasn't that I didn't care about him—I did. I cared so much that the thought of him seeing the parts of me I wasn't proud of—the parts of me that felt insecure or uncertain—terrified me. I feared that if he indeed saw me, he would realize I wasn't as perfect as I tried to appear and would eventually leave. So, I kept a part of myself hidden, thinking that if I stayed guarded, I could avoid the pain of rejection.

But by doing so, I also avoided the possibility of real intimacy. I kept him from fully knowing me, and in turn, I kept myself from fully experiencing the love he was offering. Eventually, the relationship ended, not because of a lack of love but because I was too afraid to let it deepen.

That experience taught me that intimacy does not happen when we present a perfect version of ourselves but when we allow ourselves to be vulnerable. It happens when we are brave enough to let someone see us as we are and when we trust that they will love us, not despite our imperfections but because of them.

YOUR FEAR OF INTIMACY: WHERE ARE YOU HOLDING BACK?

Now, I invite you to reflect on your relationships. Where are you holding back from true intimacy? Do you hide a part of yourself, afraid that if someone sees the real you, they might pull away? Are there moments when you deflect, avoid, or change the subject when things get too personal?

The fear of intimacy is subtle, often showing up in ways we don't immediately recognize. We may be open and loving on the surface but hesitate to share our more profound thoughts, feelings, and insecurities. We may fear being seen fully because we believe that if someone knew the whole of who we are, they wouldn't love us as much.

But here's the truth: intimacy requires vulnerability. It requires the willingness to be seen fully, not just the parts of ourselves that we think are lovable, but also the parts we're unsure about. The deeper the intimacy, the greater the connection. And while it can be scary to let someone in, the reward is a relationship built on trust, authenticity, and love.

EXERCISE: MOVING TOWARD INTIMACY

Let's take some time to explore how you can move past the fear of intimacy and open yourself up to deeper connections. This exercise will guide you through identifying where you're holding back and how to practice vulnerability in your relationships.

1. **Identify Where You're Guarded**: Think about a relationship where you've been holding back emotionally. This could be a romantic partner, a close friend, or even a family member. Write down how you've been guarding your heart—avoiding specific conversations, downplaying your feelings, or keeping a part of yourself hidden.

2. **Acknowledge the Fear**: What is the fear that's keeping you from fully opening up? Are you afraid of being judged? Are you worried that if the other person sees your vulnerabilities, they won't love you as much? Be honest with yourself about the fears that are holding you back.

3. **Start Small**: Intimacy doesn't happen all at once—it's built over time through small acts of vulnerability. Choose one small thing you can share with the person that feels vulnerable but manageable. It could be sharing a personal story, expressing an insecurity, or opening up about how you're feeling emotionally.

4. **Observe the Response**: After you've shared, observe

how the other person responds. Did they listen with empathy and understanding? When we open up, we often create a space for deeper connection, and the other responds with care and support.

5. **Practice Regularly**: Vulnerability, like any skill, requires practice. The more you allow yourself to be open and honest in your relationships, the more comfortable you'll become with intimacy. Make a habit of sharing your thoughts and feelings regularly rather than waiting for the "right" moment.

This exercise is about taking small steps toward vulnerability and intimacy. Gradually opening up creates a foundation of trust and connection in your relationships.

THE FEAR OF REJECTION: WHY WE PROTECT OURSELVES

At the heart of the fear of intimacy is often the fear of rejection. We worry that if someone sees us fully—the parts we usually keep hidden—they will judge us, pull away, or decide we're not enough. This fear can lead us to maintain emotional distance in relationships, protecting us from potential hurt and preventing us from experiencing true love and connection.

But here's the paradox: we often create the distance we fear by keeping people at arm's length to avoid rejection. Intimacy requires risk. It requires us to be vulnerable and trust that the other person will accept us, flaws and all. And while there's always the possibility of rejection, there's also the possibility of more profound love, understanding, and connection.

In my life, I've found that the fear of rejection is often worse than the reality. When I've allowed myself to be vulnerable in relationships—when I've shared my insecurities, admitted my fears, and let someone see the real me—I've often been met with more love and understanding than I expected. The fear of rejection is real, but it doesn't have to control us. By embracing vulnerability, we open ourselves up to the possibility of more profound, more fulfilling relationships.

PRACTICAL WISDOM: EMBRACING INTIMACY AS A PATH TO DEEPER LOVE

Intimacy is vital to deep, meaningful relationships but requires courage and vulnerability. Here are some practical ways to embrace intimacy in your relationships and move past the fear of being indeed seen:

1. **Be Honest About Your Feelings**: Emotional honesty is one of the most important aspects of intimacy. Practice being honest instead of hiding your feelings or pretending everything is fine. If you're feeling scared, insecure, or uncertain, express those emotions to the person you're close to. Vulnerability is the foundation of intimacy.

2. **Allow Yourself to Receive Love**: Many struggle with receiving love, especially when they don't feel worthy. Practice allowing yourself to receive love and care from others, even when it feels uncomfortable. Trust that you deserve love just as you deserve it.

3. **Challenge Negative Beliefs About Yourself**: The fear of intimacy is often rooted in adverse beliefs about ourselves—beliefs that we're not enough, that we're unworthy of love, or that we'll be rejected if someone truly sees us. Challenge these beliefs by reminding

yourself that you are worthy of love and connection, regardless of your imperfections.

4. **Take Small Risks**: Intimacy doesn't require grand gestures—it's built through small, consistent acts of vulnerability. Practice taking small emotional risks in your relationships by sharing thoughts, feelings, or memories. Over time, these small risks build trust and deepen the connection.

5. **Trust the Process**: Intimacy is a process, not a destination. Building trust and emotional closeness in relationships takes time. Be patient with yourself and the other person as you navigate the path to a deeper connection. Trust that with time, vulnerability will lead to greater love and understanding.

EXERCISE: BUILDING INTIMACY THROUGH VULNERABILITY

Here's an exercise designed to help you build intimacy in your relationships by embracing vulnerability:

1. **Choose a Relationship to Deepen**: Think of one relationship where you want to build intimacy and connection. This could be with a partner, a close friend, or a family member.

2. **Identify a Fear You've Been Holding Onto**: Reflect on a fear or insecurity you've been holding back from sharing in this relationship. It could be something you're afraid to reveal because you worry about being judged or misunderstood.

3. **Share with Vulnerability**: Set aside time to converse honestly with this person. Share your fear or insecurity in a way that feels vulnerable but safe. For example, you might say, *"I've been feeling insecure about this, and I wanted to talk to you about it."* Allow yourself to be fully seen.

4. **Listen to Their Response**: After you've shared, listen to how the other person responds. Often, vulnerability invites empathy and deeper connection; the other person will likely respond with care and understanding.

5. **Reflect on the Experience**: After the conversation,

reflect on how it felt to be vulnerable. Did it deepen your connection? Did it bring a sense of relief? Use this reflection to guide future conversations and continue building intimacy.

This exercise helps you take small steps toward vulnerability, creating a foundation of trust and emotional closeness in your relationships.

REFLECTION: THE FREEDOM OF TRUE INTIMACY

The fear of intimacy can feel overwhelming, but it doesn't have to control our relationships. When we allow ourselves to be vulnerable and let someone see us fully, we open the door to deeper, more meaningful connections. Intimacy is not about perfection—it's about authenticity. It's about being brave enough to say, *"This is who I am,"* and trusting that we are worthy of love just as we are.

As you progress in your relationships, I encourage you to embrace intimacy as a path to more profound love and connection. Allow yourself to be seen for the parts of you that feel safe, not just for who you are. The more you practice vulnerability, the more you'll experience the richness of true intimacy and the freedom that comes with it.

MEMORABLE QUOTE:

"Intimacy is the courage to be fully seen, knowing that we are worthy of love in our vulnerability."

THE POWER OF FEAR TO TRANSFORM

"On the other side of fear is growth, freedom, and the realization that you are far stronger than you ever imagined."

As we come to the end of this journey together, I want to remind you of a truth that has been woven throughout these pages: Fear is not your enemy. It is your ally in the journey toward growth and self-discovery. The voice calls you to step beyond what is comfortable, embrace what is uncertain, and trust in your strength.

One message I hope you take away from this book is that fear is not something to be eliminated or conquered—it is something to be embraced. The presence of fear in your life is not a sign that you are on the wrong path; it is a signal that you are on the brink of something new, something that has the potential to change you in ways you cannot yet imagine.

Throughout this book, we have explored the many ways in which fear manifests in our lives. From the fear of vulnerability that keeps us from deepening our relationships to the fear of failure that prevents us from pursuing our dreams, fear shows up in the moments that matter most. But as we've learned, it is precisely in these moments that we have the opportunity to grow.

You now have the tools to navigate fear with courage and grace. You know that fear is not something to avoid but to move through. You understand that each time you face your fear, you become more resilient, courageous, and aligned with your true self.

But this journey doesn't end here. Fear will continue to show up in your life, as it does for all of us. The key is not to try to avoid fear but to recognize it, to listen to what it's telling you, and to use it as a guide for growth. The next time you feel fear rising within you, I encourage you to ask yourself: *What is this fear trying to teach me? What door is it asking me to walk through?*

Fear is the signpost on the road to growth. It is the discomfort we feel when stretching beyond what is known, and it is the catalyst that pushes us toward our potential. Every outstanding achievement, every profound connection, every personal transformation begins with a moment of fear. And it is in those moments that we are given the choice: to retreat into comfort or to step forward into growth.

I invite you to continue choosing growth. Choose the path that leads you through fear and into the life you are meant to live. Trust in your ability to navigate the unknown, and know that you are growing stronger, braver, and more aligned with your purpose whenever you face your fear.

You have everything you need within you to face whatever fears come your way. You dare to be vulnerable, have the strength to overcome setbacks, and the resilience to keep moving forward, even when the path is uncertain. This is the power of fear—to transform you, to guide you, and to bring you closer to the life you are meant to live.

Thank you for walking this journey with me. May you continue to embrace fear as the catalyst for growth that it is, and may you live a rich, meaningful life filled with the courage to become who you indeed are.

This is not the end—it is only the beginning.

CHAPTER 11: THE FEAR OF BEING ENOUGH: DISCOVERING YOUR WORTH

Introduction: The Quiet Fear That Holds Us Back

"At the root of so many of our fears is the quiet, persistent voice that asks: Am I enough? But the truth is, you have always been enough, and it's time to believe that."

There's a fear that we don't always talk about. It doesn't scream or shout; it whispers. The quiet fear exists in the background of our minds, affecting how we see ourselves and the world around us. It's the fear that we'll never be enough no matter what we do or how hard we try.

This fear manifests in many aspects of our lives. It appears when we hesitate to speak up, thinking our voice doesn't matter. It arises when we shy away from opportunities, believing we don't deserve success. It creeps in when we compare ourselves to others, convinced we'll never measure up. This fear—often deeply ingrained from past experiences, societal expectations, or self-doubt—keeps us from fully embracing our potential.

But here's the truth: You have always been enough. The journey isn't about becoming enough; it's about rediscovering and accepting who you already are. The fear of not being enough can be overcome by achieving more but by recognizing your intrinsic worth and honoring who you indeed are.

This chapter will explore the fear of not being enough, how it holds us back, and how we can learn to cultivate self-worth and confidence. This isn't about proving ourselves to the world—it's about embracing our true selves and knowing, deep down, that we are worthy of love, success, and happiness just as we are.

MY STORY: THE CONSTANT STRUGGLE FOR PERFECTION

I spent many years believing that I would finally be enough if I could do everything perfectly. I might finally feel worthy if I could be the perfect mother, partner, and professional. But no matter how hard I tried, it always felt like I was falling short. There was always something more to achieve, something more to prove.

One of the clearest memories of this struggle was during a close friend's birthday celebration. I wanted everything perfect—the gifts, the event, the experience. I spent weeks planning, making sure every detail was just right. But as the day approached, I found myself growing anxious and overwhelmed. I wasn't worried about whether my friend would enjoy the celebration; I was concerned about whether I had done enough.

Despite the laughter and joy all around me during the party, I couldn't shake the feeling that I hadn't done enough—that maybe I wasn't enough. Even though everyone seemed happy, I couldn't see the event's success because I was too focused on my inadequacies. It was a painful reminder of how deeply the fear of not being enough embedded into my life.

It wasn't until later, after a heartfelt conversation with that same friend, that I realized how much I had been missing out on. She expressed how grateful she was, not for the event's details, but for the thought, care, and love that went into it. She didn't see my efforts as inadequate; she saw them as meaningful. It made me reflect on how often we are our harshest critics and how the people who love us see us in a completely different light.

This moment was a turning point. I realized my worth was not tied to how perfectly I performed or how flawlessly I showed up. My worth was inherent. I was enough simply because I existed, and that was something I had to learn to believe.

YOUR FEAR OF BEING ENOUGH: WHERE DOES IT SHOW UP?

Now, I want to invite you to reflect on your own life. Where does the fear of not being enough show up for you? Is it in your work where you constantly push yourself to achieve more, hoping that success will bring you a sense of worthiness? Is it in your relationships where you worry you're not giving enough, doing enough, or being enough to be truly loved?

This fear can show up in subtle ways. Maybe you hesitate to take a risk or step into a new opportunity because you don't believe you deserve success. Perhaps you avoid confrontation or difficult conversations because you fear speaking your truth will expose your flaws. Or maybe you find yourself comparing your life to others, convinced that everyone else has it all together while you're just trying to keep up.

Whatever form it takes, the fear of not being enough keeps us from living fully. It keeps us in a cycle of doubt, insecurity, and self-criticism. But the truth is, you are enough. You have always been enough. The journey ahead is not about proving yourself to anyone but recognizing and embracing your worth.

EXERCISE: IDENTIFYING AND RELEASING THE FEAR OF NOT BEING ENOUGH

Let's take a moment to reflect on where the fear of not being enough is holding you back and how you can begin to release it.

1. **Identify Where You Feel Inadequate**: Start by thinking about one area of your life where you often feel like you're not enough. It could be in your work, your relationships, your personal goals, or even your self-image. Write down the specific thoughts or beliefs when you think about this area.

2. **Challenge the Belief**: Ask yourself: Is it true that you're not enough? Are these beliefs based on objective reality, or are they rooted in self-doubt and past experiences? Write down an alternative belief that reflects your true worth. For example, if your belief is *"I'm not successful enough,"* challenge it with, *"Success is not the measure of my worth—I am enough just as I am."*

3. **Reframe Your Self-Talk**: Pay attention to the way you speak to yourself when feelings of inadequacy arise. Are you harsh and critical, or are you kind and

compassionate? Practice reframing negative self-talk with affirming, loving language. Instead of saying, *"I'll never be good enough,"* try saying, *"I am enough, and I am growing every day."*

4. **Celebrate Your Strengths**: Take a moment to reflect on your strengths and the qualities that make you unique. Write down a list of things you're proud of—your achievements, personal growth, and how you've shown courage or resilience. This practice helps to remind you that you are enough, not because of what you do but because of who you are.

This exercise is about shifting your mindset from self-criticism to self-compassion. It's about recognizing that your worth is inherent, and you don't need to do more or be more to prove it.

THE JOURNEY TO SELF-WORTH: RELEASING COMPARISON AND EMBRACING YOUR AUTHENTIC SELF

One of the most insidious ways the fear of not being enough manifests is through comparison. We compare our lives, achievements, and appearances to those around us, convinced that everyone else is doing better, achieving more, or living a more fulfilling life. But comparison is a thief—it steals our joy and closes our eyes to the unique beauty of our journey.

The truth is, you are on your path, and it's unlike anyone else's. Your worth is not measured by how you compare to others but by how aligned you are with your authentic self. The more you let go of comparison and embrace your unique gifts, the more you will begin to see that you have always been enough.

Cultivating self-worth is a lifelong journey. It's not about reaching a point where you always feel confident—it's about learning to show up for yourself with love, compassion, and acceptance, even when you don't feel enough. It's about choosing, every day, to believe in your inherent value and to honor yourself for who you are.

PRACTICAL WISDOM: CULTIVATING SELF-WORTH AND LETTING GO OF INSECURITY

Here are some practical steps you can take to cultivate self-worth and begin to let go of the fear of not being enough:

1. **Practice Self-Compassion**: Practice speaking to yourself with kindness whenever inadequacy arises. Treat yourself like a close friend going through a tough time. Offer yourself the same empathy and understanding.

2. **Release the Need for Perfection**: Perfectionism is often rooted in the fear of not being enough. Let go of the idea that you must be perfect to be worthy. Embrace your imperfections as part of what makes you human and lovable.

3. **Celebrate Your Wins**: Make it a habit to celebrate your accomplishments, no matter how small. Each time you achieve something, take a moment to acknowledge your efforts and recognize your worth.

4. **Surround Yourself with Support**: Build a support system of people who remind you of your worth and encourage your growth. Surrounding yourself with positive, loving people can help counteract feelings of

inadequacy and insecurity.

5. **Affirm Your Worth**: Use affirmations to remind yourself of your inherent value. Try repeating affirmations like, *"I am enough," "I am worthy of love and success,"* or *"I embrace myself fully, just as I am."* These simple statements can have a powerful impact on your mindset over time.

EXERCISE: RECLAIMING YOUR WORTH

Here's an exercise designed to help you reclaim your worth and let go of the fear of not being enough:

1. **Write a Letter to Yourself**: Write a letter to yourself from someone who loves you deeply—someone who sees your worth, strengths, and unique gifts. In the letter, explain why you are enough, just as you are. This practice helps shift your perspective and remind you of your inherent value.

2. **Create a "Self-Worth" Journal**: Start a journal where you regularly write down things you're proud of, moments when you felt strong, and affirmations that reinforce your worth. This journal serves as a reminder of your growth and resilience and can help you reconnect with your self-worth on difficult days.

3. **Release the Comparison**: Whenever you compare your life to someone else's, pause and reflect on what makes your journey unique. Write down three things you're grateful for, and remind yourself that your path is yours alone.

This exercise helps you build a stronger relationship with yourself, rooted in self-love, compassion, and a deep sense of worth.

REFLECTION: YOU HAVE ALWAYS BEEN ENOUGH

As we close this chapter, I want to leave you with one final truth: You have always been enough. You don't need to achieve, do, or be more to prove your worth. Your value is inherent, and the journey ahead is about learning to believe that for yourself.

The fear of not being enough may still appear occasionally, but now you have the tools to recognize it for what it is: a fear that no longer needs to define you. Every time you embrace your worth and offer compassion, you step toward living an authentic, fulfilling life aligned with your identity.

MEMORABLE QUOTE:

"You have always been enough. The journey is not about proving your worth but learning to see and believe it."

CHAPTER 12: THE FEAR OF SUCCESS: EMBRACING YOUR POTENTIAL

Introduction: The Surprising Fear of Success

"Success isn't just about reaching your goals—it's about accepting that you can achieve more than you ever imagined."

Most of us talk about success as something we strive for and want. We set goals, work hard, and push ourselves to achieve greatness. Yet, for many of us, an unexpected fear arises as we get closer to success—a fear that feels almost contradictory. Why would we fear success when it's something we desire?

The fear of success often hides in the shadows. It's less apparent than the fear of failure or rejection, but it can be as powerful. As we move closer to achieving our dreams, questions and doubts surface: *What if I'm not ready for this? What if success changes my relationships? What if I can't sustain it?* These fears can lead us to self-sabotage, procrastinate, or shrink away from opportunities that could elevate us to the next level.

Success brings new responsibilities, visibility, and the pressure to maintain what we've built. It forces us to step into a bigger version of ourselves that may feel unfamiliar and uncomfortable. But here's the truth: you are capable of success and worthy of the opportunities that come your way.

This chapter will explore the fear of success, how it manifests in our lives, and how we can move past it to fully embrace our potential. Success is not something to be feared—it's something to be welcomed. It is the natural result of stepping into your purpose and allowing yourself to shine.

MY STORY: THE WEIGHT OF EXPECTATIONS

I vividly remember the first time I realized I was afraid of success. It was a moment I had been working toward for years —an ample opportunity that would allow me to share my work on a larger platform and reach more people than I had ever imagined. I had spent months preparing and countless hours of effort, and when the opportunity finally arrived, I was paralyzed with doubt.

Instead of feeling excited, I felt overwhelmed. The weight of expectations pressed down on me, and I began to question whether I was ready. *What if I fail at this level? What if I can't live up to the expectations? What if success changes me?* These thoughts consumed me, and for a brief moment, I considered walking away from the opportunity altogether.

I realized then that my fear wasn't about the possibility of failing but the reality of succeeding. I had become comfortable in my current level of achievement, and stepping into a bigger version of myself felt terrifying. Success would mean more visibility, responsibility, and pressure to keep performing at a high level. It would push me out of my comfort zone and force me to grow in ways I wasn't sure I was ready for.

But I also knew this opportunity was exactly what I had been working toward. I couldn't let fear hold me back. So, I made a decision: I would embrace success, even if it felt uncomfortable.

I would trust in my abilities and allow myself to step into the potential I knew existed within me.

That decision changed everything. I moved forward with the opportunity, and though there were moments of doubt, I discovered that I was far more capable than I had given myself credit for. Success didn't destroy me—it elevated me. It pushed me to grow, to challenge myself, and to become the person I was meant to be.

YOUR FEAR OF SUCCESS: HOW IS IT HOLDING YOU BACK?

Take a moment to reflect on your own life. Are there areas where you've been holding back from fully embracing your potential? Have you ever hesitated to take the next step in your career, personal development, or relationships, not because you're afraid of failure but because you're so scared of what success might bring?

The fear of success often manifests as self-sabotage. Maybe you procrastinate on a project that could lead to a promotion because you're afraid of the added responsibility. Maybe you downplay your achievements or avoid discussing your goals with others because you're worried about how they'll perceive you. Or perhaps you find yourself retreating from opportunities that could elevate you to the next level, fearing that success will change your life in ways you're not ready for.

But here's the truth: success is not something to be feared. It is the natural outcome of growth, effort, and perseverance. Success doesn't have to change you negatively—it can expand you, push you to grow, and open doors to new opportunities that align with your true potential.

EXERCISE: OVERCOMING THE FEAR OF SUCCESS

Let's take some time to explore where the fear of success might be holding you back and how you can begin to embrace your potential.

1. **Identify Where You're Holding Back**: Think about an area of your life where you've been holding back from success. It could be in your career, relationships, or a personal goal. Write down the specific ways you've been hesitating or self-sabotaging, even though you know you're capable of more.

2. **Acknowledge the Fear**: What is the fear preventing you from fully stepping into success? Are you afraid of the added responsibility? Do you worry that success will change your relationships or bring more pressure? Write down the specific fears that come up when you think about success.

3. **Reframe the Fear**: Now, challenge those fears. What if success doesn't bring more pressure but more freedom? What if success deepens your relationships by allowing you to show up as your best self? Write down new beliefs that support your ability to succeed without fear. For example, *"I am capable of handling the responsibilities that come with success,"* or *"Success will bring me opportunities that align with my purpose."*

4. **Take One Step Toward Success**: Choose one small action you can take today that moves you closer to your definition of success. It could be submitting a project, applying for a promotion, or simply acknowledging your achievements to someone you trust. The goal is to start taking steps that show you are ready to embrace success.

This exercise helps you identify and confront the fear of success while encouraging you to take proactive steps toward realizing your potential.

THE FEAR OF SUCCESS: WHY WE HOLD OURSELVES BACK

At the heart of the fear of success is often the fear of change. Success, by its very nature, changes things. It shifts our circumstances, responsibilities, and sometimes even how others perceive us. But more than that, success requires us to grow—to step into a version of ourselves that may feel unfamiliar or intimidating.

We may worry that success will make us stand out, create distance between us and the people we love, or bring new pressures that we're not ready to handle. These fears are valid, but they don't have to define us. The key is recognizing that success doesn't have to change who we are—it can simply expand our capabilities.

Success isn't about perfection or achieving everything all at once. It's about growth. It's about allowing yourself to evolve and step into your potential, even when it feels uncomfortable. The more we embrace success, the more we realize that we are capable of far more than we ever imagined.

PRACTICAL WISDOM: EMBRACING SUCCESS WITH CONFIDENCE

Here are some practical steps you can take to overcome the fear of success and embrace your full potential:

1. **Acknowledge Your Achievements**: One of the first steps to overcoming the fear of success is recognizing what you've already accomplished. Take time to reflect on your past achievements and celebrate how far you've come. This helps build confidence and reminds you that success is something you're capable of.

2. **Visualize Your Success**: Spend time visualizing what success looks like for you—not just the external achievements but the internal feelings of fulfillment and growth. Visualize yourself handling success with grace and confidence, knowing you can navigate the responsibilities that come with it.

3. **Surround Yourself with Support**: Success doesn't have to be a lonely journey. Surround yourself with people who support your growth and who will celebrate your successes with you. A solid support system can help ease the fear of success by reminding you that you're not alone.

4. **Embrace the Discomfort**: Success often requires stepping out of our comfort zones. Instead of resisting the discomfort, embrace it as a sign that you're

growing. Remember that discomfort is temporary, but the growth it brings is lasting.

5. **Trust in Your Potential**: Believe in yourself and your potential. You are capable of handling whatever success brings your way. You have the strength, resilience, and abilities to navigate the opportunities and challenges that come with success.

EXERCISE: STEPPING INTO YOUR POTENTIAL

Here's an exercise to help you embrace your potential and overcome the fear of success:

1. **Write a Success Letter to Yourself**: Imagine achieving your dream of success. Write a letter to your present self from this future version of you. In the letter, describe how success feels, what you've accomplished, and how you've grown. This exercise helps you connect with the version of yourself ready for success.

2. **Take a Small Risk**: Success often requires taking risks, even small ones. Choose one area of your life where you've been playing it safe and take a small risk that moves you closer to your goals. It could be saying yes to a new opportunity, pitching an idea, or putting yourself out there boldly.

3. **Reflect on How Success Has Shown Up**: Reflect on the small successes you've already experienced. Whether it's personal growth, professional achievements, or relationships, recognize that success isn't a destination—it's a series of moments when you step into your potential.

This exercise helps you shift your mindset from fear to excitement, allowing you to embrace success as a natural part of your growth.

REFLECTION: THE FREEDOM TO SUCCEED

Success is not something to fear—it's something to embrace. It is the result of your hard work, dedication, and courage. The fear of success may still appear, but now you know it doesn't have to hold you back. Knowing you can handle any opportunities, you have the tools to navigate success confidently.

As you continue on your journey, I encourage you to step fully into your potential. Trust that success is not just possible for you —it's inevitable when you allow yourself to shine. You are ready for success and worthy of all the opportunities and abundance that come with it.

MEMORABLE QUOTE:

"Success isn't something to fear—it's something to embrace. You are capable, and you are ready."